Swiss *movement*, English *heart*

# supercarzone.com

**Get connected today, it's quick, easy and FREE**

## Join up & join in

Local Meets

UK & European Tours

Track Day Events

Exclusive Previews

## News
Supercar news desk

## Events
Local, National & International events calendar

## Reviews
Owners personal supercar review section

## MediaZone
Video & photo event reports gallery

## TorqueZone
Forum based chat area & noticeboard

## CompareZone
Unique supercar comparisons

## InfoZone
Supercar manufacturers history & current model cars

## Games
Our very own collection of supercar online games

### Interested in Supercars?
*"SupercarZone is a free online community website, run by supercar owners and enthusiasts **exclusively for supercars**"*

### Want to participate?
*"Enjoy the company of other supercar owners and share experiences with likeminded car enthusiasts"*

### Compare & Review
*"Supercar reviews from owners with their first hand, real world experiences, day to day running, costs and true values."*

### Join In & have fun
*"Make friends and join our growing membership with events, track days, & tours all organised professionally by our partners"*

### Information & Resource Area
*"Resources and information about all the supercar leading manufacturers cars and some of the eccentric and exotic hyper cars"*

### Something for you?
*"Enjoy discounts and benefits from our sponsors and partners who help make our supercar community grow.*

**supercarzone**
Supercar enthusiasts connected

'THE IDEA WAS TO MAKE A LIGHTWEIGHT, MID-ENGINED, TWO-SEAT JAGUAR THAT WOULD ECLIPSE THE F40'

# Contents

# THE A-Z GUIDE TO SUPERCARS

## FROM THE PUBLISHERS OF evo MAGAZINE

**MagBook managing editor** Peter Tomalin
**Senior designer** Adam Shorrock
**Production editor** Ian Eveleigh
**Contributing editor** David Vivian
**Additional pictures** Magiccarpics.co.uk
**MagBook advertising sales** Rob Schulp

## MANAGEMENT

**Digital production manager** Nicky Baker
**MagBook publisher** Dharmesh Mistry
**Operations director** Robin Ryan
**MD of advertising** Julian Lloyd-Evans
**Newstrade director** David Barker
**Commercial & retail director** Martin Belson
**Editoral director** Harry Metcalfe
**Publishing director** Geoff Love
**Chief operating officer** Brett Reynolds
**Group finance director** Ian Leggett
**Chief executive** James Tye
**Chairman** Felix Dennis

# Introduction

**L**ogic says that the supercar's days should be numbered, that we're all just waiting for the economic or ecological asteroid that will consign these dinosaurs to automotive history. Thing is, supercars have never made much logical sense. And as long as there are wealthy enthusiasts to buy them, it seems there will always be brilliant engineers striving to ensure that these fabulous machines make the evolutionary leaps required to continue their survival. So we have Ferrari paring back the size and weight of its front-engined flagship to create the stunning new F12 Berlinetta, Pagani adopting turbochargers to improve the efficiency of its breathtaking Huayra, and Porsche and Jaguar developing hybrid powertrains for their forthcoming hypercars. And with McLaren readying the true successor to the F1, Planet Supercar has never looked a better place to be. Enjoy!

*Peter Tomalin, managing editor*

# Ascari KZ1

*PRETTY SHAPE, BMW V8 AND HANDLING BY EX-LOTUS ENGINEERS... THE KZ1 HAD IT ALL*

British company Ascari was formed in the mid-1990s and produced its first supercar, the Ecosse, in 1998. But it really hit its stride in the early 2000s under the ownership of multi-millionaire Dutch businessman Klaas Zwart, who had ambitious plans for roadgoing supercars, race-cars and his own race circuit and resort in Spain. The KZ1, built in a brand new factory in Banbury in the English Midlands, was his bold bid to take on the likes of Ferrari and Lamborghini.

Launched in 2003, the KZ1 used the E39 BMW M5's 5.0-litre V8. Breathed on, dry-sumped, mid-mounted and teamed with a CIMA six-speed manual gearbox, it developed 500bhp and allowed Ascari to attach some impressive performance claims to the all-carbonfibre, 1300kg KZ1: 0-60mph in less than 4sec and a top speed of 200mph, figures that looked even better when viewed

## SPECIFICATION

| | |
|---|---|
| Years made | 2003-2010 |
| Engine | V8, 4941cc |
| Max power | 500bhp @7000rpm |
| Torque | 368lb ft @4800rpm |
| 0-60mph | 3.8sec |
| Max speed | 200mph |
| Price | £235,000 (new) c£50-100,000 (today) |

**evo** RATING
★★★★☆

in context with the double wishbone suspension and AP Racing brakes.

A compact, pretty car, with a delicacy and stance not unlike that of a Ferrari 360, the KZ1 was nevertheless its own car. When **evo**'s John Barker got behind the wheel, he was impressed by the quality but even more taken with the chassis, detecting hints of Esprit Sport 350 in its clean, crisp steering and tightly controlled roll and pitch. As Lotus engineers had been involved with the car's development, perhaps it wasn't such a surprise. The KZ1 could also be set up more or less to customers' individual requirements.

The bespoke tailoring certainly helped its cause but the KZ1 was formidably expensive in a world that could offer a V10 Audi R8 for less than half the KZ1's price. Despite launching more powerful, track-oriented versions – the A10 and KZ1-R – sales only limped into double figures, and today Zwart concentrates on the Ascari resort and his racing interests.

Left: cockpit was neat and well-finished. Above: 5-litre V8 from E39 M5 was tuned to 500bhp

# Aston Martin V8 Vantage

## AS ITALIAN SUPERCARS BECAME WIDER AND LOWER, THIS WAS A VERY BRITISH RESPONSE

**B**y the mid-'70s, Italy must have reckoned it had the supercar blueprint sussed: mid-mounted V12 with eye-popping power claims; bodywork sub-contracted to brilliant young designers given free rein to work out their fantasies; a fusion of beauty, technical braggadocio and aural drama the like of which we'd never seen. Then, in 1977, Britain rolled out its response, and it was wonderfully straightforward.

Aston Martin blanked off the grille and bonnet scoop of its V8 coupe. The effect was remarkable. The old Newport Pagnell-built bruiser, which had been around since the turn of the decade, suddenly took on the aura of an assassin with urgent scores to settle. Of course, it's what that grille signified that made it such a feared vision in the low rear-view mirrors of the Latin exotica. Britain had its first supercar.

With skimmed heads, bigger valves,

reprofiled cams and 48IDA carburettors, the 5.3-litre V8 now developed 390bhp, good enough for 0-60mph in 5.3sec (a tenth quicker than a Ferrari Daytona), 170mph flat-out and a side order of Lamborghini frittata for breakfast.

The suspension was stiffened and lowered, too, with wider rubber to put the extra power to good use. Of course, the grille blanking plate's true purpose was to cut drag and hence increase the top speed to Countach-worrying levels, air flow instead being fed under the bumper, so full cooling was retained.

The Vantage flew the flag for Britain for more than a decade before it was finally retired in 1989. In 1986 the V8 was made even mightier, with bigger carbs and racing-type cylinder heads helping boost the output to 427bhp – essentially the same engine that would power the Vantage Zagato (ovreleaf). Subtle as a Henry Cooper left hook maybe but, as far as the Italian supercar establishment was concerned, the result was much the same.

### SPECIFICATION

**Years made**
1977-1989
**Engine** V8, 5340cc
**Max power** 390bhp
@ 5000rpm
**Torque** n/a
**0-60mph** 5.3sec
**Max speed** 170mph
**Price** £20,000 (new),
c£40-100,000 (today)

### evo RATING
★★★☆☆

Left: 5.3 litres of prime British V8. Opposite: blanked-off grilles helped increase Vantage's top speed

WRE 816S

# Aston Martin V8 Vantage Zagato

*IN THE MID-'80S, ITALIAN DESIGN HOUSE ZAGATO PUT ITS UNIQUE STAMP ON THE VANTAGE*

**I**talian design house Zagato definitely went through a 'less is more' period in the '80s. You could see it in Lancia's Integrale-based Hyena, and the same sense of sucked-in, condensed, hard-bodied minimalism is evident in its 1986 take on the V8 Vantage for long-time client Aston Martin. Pretty it wasn't (and with the sublime 1960s DB4 GT Zagato in the back catalogue, that was a disappointment to some) but it still looks remarkably modern today, a design devoid of the grand stylistic gestures that can date so quickly.

In some respects, the project reprised the lightweight DB4 GT Zagato. Like its classic counterpart, the modern V8 Vantage Zagato was reduced in overall size and clothed with an aluminum body from Italy. As with the DB4, the chassis was shortened and the rear seats removed, the result being a considerably more agile and involving device for keen drivers. Fans included Aston enthusiast Rowan Atkinson, who bought the first right-hand-drive example and later had it converted into a 482bhp race-car. By the end of the '80s, in the height of the supercar boom, examples were changing hands for as much as £450,000.

In all, 52 examples of the coupe were produced, followed by 37 Volante convertible versions. The Volante made its debut at the 1987 Geneva Auto Show and was offered at an even more limited run of only 25, although a total of 37 were eventually made due to high demand. Styling changes included flip-up front headlight covers and the removal of the coupe's huge bonnet bulge.

So one of the finest Astons in pure driving terms, and one that despite its (at the time) controversial looks has aged rather well. Aston has rekindled its relationship with Zagato in recent years, the latest collaboration being a version of the current V8 Vantage.

### SPECIFICATION

| | |
|---|---|
| Years made | 1986-1990 |
| Engine | V8, 5340cc |
| Max power | 432bhp @5000rpm |
| Torque | 395lb ft @5100rpm |
| 0-60mph | 4.9sec |
| Max speed | 186mph |
| Price | £87,000 (new), £100-150,000 (now) |

**evo** RATING
★★★★☆

Left: open-top Volante version was even rarer than the coupe (main pic) and did without its large bonnet bulge

# Aston Martin Bulldog

## ONLY ONE BULLDOG WAS BUILT, BUT THIS ASTON HYPERCAR STILL HAS THE POWER TO SHOCK

I n the light of everything that's happened since 1979, perhaps the Bulldog wasn't such a daft idea after all. Aston's Veyron. Designed by setsquare-loving William Towns soon after finishing the equally angular AM Lagonda, the Bulldog was, arguably, the world's first 'hypercar'.

It was huge but low (just 43 inches road-to-roof), it had powered gullwing doors, digital instruments and – way ahead of its time, this – a reversing TV camera. No one really cared about that, though. The Bulldog's greater act of prescience was that cars would one day have monstrous power outputs and top speeds higher than those of light aircraft.

The initial engineering work was carried out by AML chief engineer Mike Loasby; the codename for the project was DP K9, after the robot dog in the Doctor Who television show. When Loasby went to work for DeLorean in 1979, Keith Martin

**SPECIFICATION**

**Years made** 1979
**Engine** V8, 5340cc, twin-turbo
**Max power** 600bhp @6200rpm
**Torque** 500lb ft @5000rpm
**0-60mph** 5.1sec
**Max speed** 237mph
**Price** £130,000 (new), c£1,000,000 (today)

**evo** RATING
★★★★☆

spent the next three years finishing the project and carrying out the initial testing, including high-speed laps of MIRA.

Bulldog's Bosch-injected twin-turbocharged version of the classic 5.3-litre Aston Martin V8 was reputed to have hit over 700bhp on the test bench but this was wound down to a claimed 600bhp once installed.

Although a cosy two-seater, everything about the car was XXL, including the Pirelli P7-shod Compomotive split-rim alloys which boasted a 345/35-sized footprint at the back. Claimed top speed was a, back then, completely absurd 237mph. Whether that was in any way realistic we'll never know as the best it every managed at MIRA (far from ideal) was 192mph.

Twenty-five Bulldogs were planned but only one, a left-hooker, was ever made – after the car had been unveiled to the press at Aston Clinton, it was sold for a reputed £130,000. Last year the Bulldog emerged again for sale at $1,300,000.

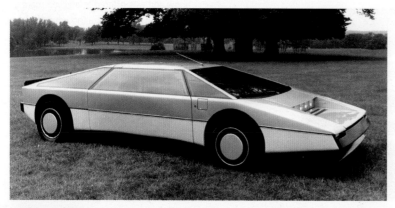

Bulldog looked like a concept car, but it was fully functioning. Left: nose panel dropped to reveal a battery of headlamps

# Aston Martin Virage Vantage

*THROUGH THE 1990s, ASTON'S FLAGSHIP WAS THIS TWIN-SUPERCHARGED HEAVYWEIGHT*

**T**he Virage Vantage was the valedictory blast for old-school Aston, a glorious, evolving celebration of bulk versus brute force. Developed from the slightly underwhelming Virage coupe, which had replaced the classic V8 in 1989, the new Vantage's pumped-up bodywork and no-nonsense attitude made it a real hero car to a whole generation of British sports car fans.

In its original 1993 form, its quad-cam, 32-valve, 5.3-litre V8, aided by two superchargers, heaved out 550bhp and 550lb ft of torque. Unsurprisingly, it would become known as the V550. It could do 186mph and hit 60mph from rest in 4.5sec, proving that, although it weighed the best part of two tons, a big engine would always get the upper hand – in a straight line at least.

Just to make absolutely sure, Aston uprated the engine to 600bhp and

600lb ft in 1998 (yes, the V600), elevating the claimed top speed to 202mph and cutting the 0-60mph time to 3.9sec. Seldom had anything so heavy moved quite so quickly. Even more surprising, however, was the urgency with which the Vantage could be hustled through bends. Sure, the huge tyres screamed for mercy, but the solution was usually to give the throttle a big old prod to induce a fluid, smoky drift that was far more satisfying than it was painful. When it came to chassis balance, the Aston was easily the equal of Ferrari's 456.

Forty Le Mans-badged cars were made in 1999 (604bhp, stiffer suspension, upgraded interior, Le Mans-winning DBR-1 aping cosmetics) to send the Vantage on its way and close a remarkable chapter in the Aston story.

It was replaced in 2000 by the all-new Vanquish model, which ushered in the start of a new era for the marque; we would never see the like of the brutish but rather wonderful Vantage again.

## SPECIFICATION

**Years made** 1993-1999
**Engine** V8, 5340cc, twin superchargers
**Max power** 550bhp @6500rpm (V550)
**Torque** 550lb ft @4000rpm (V550)
**0-60mph** 4.5sec
**Max speed** 186mph
**Price** £87,000 (new), £50-100,000 (today)

**evo RATING**
★★★★☆

In 1998, Aston introduced the V600 version, so named because peak power had increased from 550 to 600bhp

# Aston Martin Vanquish

## AS ASTON ENTERED A NEW MILLENNIUM, IT NEEDED AN ALL-NEW SUPERCAR. CUE VANQUISH!

A ll right, any of the current Aston line-up (Rapide included) would kick the Vanquish into touch for chassis dynamics. Yet there's still something magnificent and deeply desirable about this car, especially in its later, more potent, S guise. For style and sonics, Aston has produced nothing better since its 2007 demise.

The Ian Callum-penned Vanquish saw Aston Martin leaving behind the years of magnificent denial (the Virage Vantage had more dinosaur DNA than anything in Jurassic Park) to get with the new-tech programme. It was truly transitional, the last car to be hand-built at Newport Pagnell but with the extruded, bonded aluminium and composite 'VH' chassis architecture found beneath the skin of all subsequent Astons.

It had a shaky start. Slated to make its debut at the 2000 Birmingham Motor Show, it was pulled at the 11th hour by

**SPECIFICATION**

**Years made** 2001-2007
**Engine** V12, 5935cc
**Max power** 520bhp
@7000rpm (S)
**Torque** 425lb ft
@5800rpm (S)
**0-60mph** 4.5sec
**Max speed** 200mph
**Price** £163,600 (new),
c£50-80,000 (today)

**evo RATING**
★★★★½

new Aston boss Dr Ulrich Bez, who took an understandable dislike to the idea of Aston's £164,000 flagship wearing facia air vents lifted from a Ford Ka. Callum was given the task of rendering the interior ambience more 'bespoke', and by the time it was production-ready, there wasn't such a jarring disconnect between the brutal beauty of the exterior and the bold, faux aluminium-adorned cabin.

Under the bonnet, a massaged version of the 48-valve 5.9-litre V12 from the DB7 Vantage had a 7 per cent increase in power and 2.5 per cent more torque.

But if 460bhp seemed more than adequate at launch, the Aston's rivals were soon unpacking bigger numbers which, in turn, forced a reality check on the Vanquish. The more muscular and tautly-suspended 'S' took care of that, with a 60bhp hike in output. The beefier brakes that came with the optional Sports Dynamic Pack were a must-have, too. Finally, Aston could roll out a worthy rival for the Ferrari 550 Maranello.

Left and opposite: 'S' version gave the Vanquish the extra muscle to match its looks and glorious V12 soundtrack

# Aston Martin V12 Vantage

## SMALL CAR, BIG ENGINE, HUGE PERFORMANCE... AND SIMPLY ONE OF THE BEST ASTONS EVER

With the 5.9-litre V12 engine from the DB9 and DBS squeezed into the compact Vantage bodyshell, the engineers at Gaydon created a truly wonderful car.

It seemed almost absurd that a body so small should be packing over 500bhp. But the V12V quickly went from fantasy to production reality, distinguished from regular Vantages by bonnet vents to help cool that giant engine. And a quick look at the tread pattern of the tyres and the aerodynamic tweaks lifted straight from the N24 race programme showed that this wasn't just intended to be some straight-line monster.

Power delivery was smooth, the gearchange slick and the ride unexpectedly supple. Obviously, with all the weight of the engine up front (the V12 is 100kg heavier than the 4.7-litre V8), the ride was still firm – but not nearly as firm as that of a rival like the Porsche

911 GT2. Hit the Sport button, located in front of the gearlever, and the throttle response became even sharper and the bellowing from the exhausts still louder by opening the baffles.

Aston struck gold with the Vantage V12. In a way it's the car we always hoped the V8 would be, with a decent ride, proper performance and engaging handling. When you add this to classic Aston lines, it's a dream ticket. After driving it in company with an Audi R8

V10, Corvette ZR1 and Porsche 911 GT3, *evo*'s John Barker remarked: 'This is clearly the best Aston the company has ever made for people like us.' Finally, Ulrich Bez had fulfilled his ambition of building an Aston Martin that could go toe-to-toe with the best from Porsche.

That's been borne out by the following the V12V enjoys among hardcore Aston fans, reflected in unusually strong residuals on the secondhand market. A modern classic if ever there was.

### SPECIFICATION

**Years made** 2009-
**Engine** V12, 5935cc
**Max power** 510bhp @6500rpm
**Torque** 420lb ft @5750rpm
**0-60mph** 4.4sec
**Max speed** 190mph
**Price** £135,000 (new), c£80-£120,000 (used)

**evo** RATING
★★★★★

# Aston Martin DBS

*INITIALLY SEEN AS A DB9 IN A BODYKIT, THE DBS HAS EMERGED AS A STAR IN ITS OWN RIGHT*

**A** DB9 with a bodykit, more power, stiffer suspension and ceramic brakes? Or a fitting flagship for Aston Martin after the Vanquish ceased production in 2007?

The DB9 had never lacked for power but, in the DBS, its 5.9-litre V12 – hand-assembled at Aston Martin's dedicated engine facility in Cologne – featured a number of grunt-enhancing modifications, including a 'by-pass' air intake port that opened above 5500rpm to allow more air into the engine, and re-profiled air inlet ports that further improved airflow into the combustion chambers. Combined with a compression ratio of 10.9:1, the results claimed by Aston were 510bhp, a 191mph top speed and 0-62mph in 4.3sec – all top-drawer supercar stuff commensurate with a £160K price tag.

Then there was the adaptive damping developed in conjunction with Bilstein; beefier springs, suspension bushes and anti-roll bars; standard carbon-

DBS's special status was boosted by roles in not one but two Bond films, Casino Royale and Quantum of Solace

## SPECIFICATION

**Years made** 2007-
**Engine** V12, 5935cc
**Max power** 510bhp @6500rpm
**Torque** 420lb ft @5750rpm
**0-60** 4.2sec
**Max speed** 191mph
**Price** £180,182 (new), c£70-135,000 (used)

**evo** RATING
★★★★½

ceramic brakes; bespoke Pirelli P Zero Corsas. The DBS was clearly a whole different proposition to the DB9, and this was reflected in its handling – taut, responsive, and with a lairy side to its character that demanded respect and rewarded commitment.

And, in the best GT tradition, the combination of sublimely effortless V12 shove, a gigantic top-gear stride and a supremely comfortable cabin was capable of simply blowing away the miles.

# Aston Martin One-77

## ASTON'S HYPERCAR HAS ALL THE CREDENTIALS TO COMPETE WITH BUGATTI AND PAGANI

When the £1.2million One-77 revealed itself to the world at the 2009 Geneva show, it did so as a naked rolling chassis, more engineering sculpture than car. After seeing it, one customer asked if he could buy two, a proper car to drive and an unskinned version to park in his living room... It is certainly one of the most beautifully detailed and constructed cars ever to see the light of day, from its carbonfibre monocoque to its hand-beaten aluminium body panels.

The engine started out as the 5.9-litre V12 from the DB9, but the only common part is the timing chain. Dry-sumped, bored out to a massive 7.3 litres, and put on an obsessive weight-saving regime, the Cosworth-developed V12 ended up weighing just 260kg and producing a quoted 750bhp, the highest figure, says Aston, for any naturally aspirated road car engine. It has a smaller flywheel to aid rev characteristics and intake variable valve timing. It's also mounted entirely behind the front axle line, making the One-77 genuinely front/mid-engined. No independent figures have been taken, but Aston claims 0-60mph in under 3.7sec and a top speed 'in excess of 220mph'.

You have to see the One-77 to believe just how ground-hugging it is. The move to a dry sump means the V12 is mounted 100mm lower in the chassis, dropping the centre of gravity massively and allowing the driver to sit that much lower too.

Production has been limited to just 77 cars, each taking around two months to build. The front wings alone are entirely hand-crafted from a single sheet of aluminium, each taking one man three weeks. Creating the 180kg carbon tub is another three-week job. So far, Aston has refused to sanction any test drives of the One-77, so final judgement will have to wait, but a genuine Aston hypercar? Surely that much is beyond doubt.

Left: inside and out, the One-77 takes familiar Aston design themes and stretches them into something far more exotic

# Aston Martin Vanquish

## THE 2013 VANQUISH IS CRITICAL FOR ASTON. CAN IT REPEAT THE MAGIC OF THE ORIGINAL?

Remember the first time you saw the original Vanquish? Probably when it was glinting on a show stand at Geneva in 2001, dropping jaws and opening wallets. It just looked so glamorous, so effortlessly cool, a world away from the Virage line that went before and a brave new chapter for a company finally on its way to stability.

Well, that was 11 years ago, and Aston hasn't made a radical styling move since, despite breaking out into new sectors and taking on everything from 911s to Ferrari 599s to Bentley Flying Spurs. There's a real sense that it's time for the company to make another giant leap forward to secure its future and to capture the imagination of the buying public again. Aston knows it too, and dusting off the Vanquish name for its new range-topper is a bold statement. Can that fabulous badge rejuvenate the company once more?

The key details are promising – full

New carbonfibre-bodied Vanquish sees a further evolution of the Aston design themes, and a 565bhp version of the superb 5.9-litre V12 engine

carbonfibre bodywork, a 25 per cent stiffer chassis than the DBS with 75 per cent new parts, a reworked V12 mounted 13mm lower, a storming 565bhp and 457lb ft, a price of £189,995, a car that 'points to an exciting and confident future'. On the other hand, it's hard to escape the feeling that the Vanquish looks like the DBS with a boot spoiler and some slightly better-defined rear haunches. It's another handsome Aston, but radical it ain't.

On the road you can sense the lighter, stiffer chassis. The steering is smoother, the whole car more in tune with the surface, less edgy than the DBS, hooked-up and agile, the Adaptive Damping System (ADS) doing its stuff. On the motorway, save for quite a lot of road noise, the Vanquish does the bewitching big-lunged GT thing perfectly. Moving onto B-roads, it seems to make a pretty good fist of being a sports car, too...

It's quick all right. The sustained, intensifying run to the limiter is a clear

# Aston Martin Vanquish

step on from the DBS. This isn't a great hammer of an engine that overwhelms the rear tyres with torque. It likes revs and now it really has an appetite above 5500rpm, the point where the DBS starts to feel a bit strangled. It can't match the sheer lunacy of Ferrari's new F12, nor is it as thrilling as the scalpel-sharp 458, but 565bhp in 1739kg is just about enough to pass for supercar status in these mind-bending times. Certainly it's rare that you feel short-changed by the 5.9-litre V12.

However, you always feel mildly disappointed with the Touchtronic 2 transmission – a six-speed ZF torque-converter automatic with paddle-shift. Around town it's refined and slips into the background, but it lacks the creamy seamlessness of the new-generation ZF eight-speed automatic. Aston says there'll be no manual option. Other details irk a little too: the seats lack support, while the satnav graphics look cheap.

So the new Vanquish struggles to compete with the F12 Berlinetta, but maybe it doesn't have to. It is a very different character to the F12 – more laid-back, less flashy and without the

Top: aggressive-looking 'aero' distinguishes the new generation Vanquish, but will it be enough?

## SPECIFICATION

**Years made** 2012-
**Engine** V12, 5935cc
**Power** 565bhp
@6750rpm
**Torque** 457lb ft
@5500rpm
**0-60mph** 4.0sec
**Top speed** 183mph
**Price** £189,995

**evo** RATING
★★★★½

F1 baggage. Although it might be a little old-fashioned in comparison to the new Ferrari, it's still highly capable and genuinely exciting.

In terms of damping, balance, agility and progressiveness, the Vanquish is effectively a new car and a much better one than the DBS. It's a good news story in an uncertain time for Aston Martin. Frustratingly, it's a story that may pass most casual observers by. If only they'd gone further with the styling...

# Audi R8 V10

*COULD AN AUDI REALLY BE AS THRILLING TO DRIVE AS A FERRARI OR LAMBO? YOU BETCHA*

Audi has some fine performance cars in its illustrious history – and a performance legend in the shape of the rally-bred Quattro. But until recently it had never really dabbled in the supercar arena. That began to change when it launched the original, V8-engined R8 in 2006. The R8 took extraneous behaviour – all the little fidgets, squirms, structure-born shudders and sundry expressions of strain and imbalance – clean out of the driving experience. What was left was pure and direct. So stiff was the structure you were strapped into and so geometrically correct the actions of its chassis that the sense of oneness was almost overwhelming.

But it still wasn't quite the real deal. The breakthrough came when the engineers took the R8 and installed a glorious V10 engine. Not since the Honda NSX had there been a supercar that was quite so useable and easy to live with.

Visually there wasn't much to get excited about, though the side-scoops were kicked out to grab more air and give more shape to the flanks, while the intakes front and rear had gappier spars and there were new crinkly 19in alloys. No, it was the 518bhp 5.2-litre V10 engine that moved the R8 up the credibility rankings, taking its performance into pukka supercar territory. Of course, it also added a more intriguing, exotic soundtrack, erupting into life with a lightly silenced, nasally *whoop*.

To go with the more muscular engine there was a sharper, more dialled-in chassis. And when Audi replaced the fixed top with a fabric roof – no folding hard-tops here – to produce the Spyder, the usual soft-top compromises (extra weight, a loss of rigidity and handling precision) largely failed to materialise, leaving just the usual open-air delights and clearer aural access to the thrilling exertions of a mighty engine.

## SPECIFICATION

**Years made** 2010-
**Engine** V10, 5204cc
**Max power** 518bhp @8000rpm
**Torque** 391lb ft @6500rpm
**0-60mph** 3.8sec
**Max speed** 196mph
**Price** £108,040 (coupe, new), £70-95,000 (used)

**evo** RATING
★★★★★

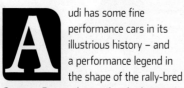

Above: crinkly 19in alloys were unique to the V10 version. Left: a typically Audi take on a supercar interior

OY09 VKE

# B. Engineering Edonis

## THE BUGATTI EB110'S WICKED HALF-BROTHER, THE EDONIS WASN'T FOR THE FAINT-HEARTED

**W**hat's the most exciting supercar no-one's ever heard of? Well, the Edonis has to be in with a shout. Italian company B. Engineering created this extraordinary supercar from leftover Bugatti EB110 chassis and engines after the early-1990s iteration of Bugatti folded (the B stood for Bugatti, and the staff included several ex-factory personnel).

Ditching the EB110's four-wheel drive and adding two large turbos in place of the donor car's four smaller units made for a truly savage creation, and the Edonis had the looks to match, with a body seemingly constructed entirely out of cooling ducts.

But then the Edonis's startling appearance is just one reason why it deserves to be remembered with a degree of awe and affection. Another was its exquisite steering. The Edonis changed direction like a Ferrari F40 – with sublime precision and beautifully judged feel. Few supercars since have had a finer helm.

And then there was the utter brutality of its twin-turbocharged 3.8-litre V12, enlarged from the EB110's 3.5 litres. So savage, sudden and relentless was the contribution of its IHI blowers, the Edonis was quite capable of ambushing the driver's senses and slapping them silly. Indeed, as the turbos spooled up, the step-change in accelerative thrust was unsettling to the point of disorientation. And just when you thought it had dumped the lot in the small of your back, there was yet more to come. More throttle, more brain-scrambling push. Added to which, the multi-layered howl of the barely soundproofed V12 was almost frightening. The EB110 was never like this.

The production target was just 21 cars though whether that number was ever sold remains in doubt. Very few have ever appeared on the secondhand market – the last was advertised for £1m euros. Not for everyone, the mad, bad Edonis...

### SPECIFICATION

**Years made** 2001-2006
**Engine** V12, 3760cc, twin-turbo
**Max power** 680bhp @8000rpm
**Torque** 542lb ft @3200rpm
**0-60mph** 3.8sec
**Max speed** 227mph
**Price** c£450,000 (new)

**evo** RATING
★★★★☆

Above: the eye of the storm. Left: a body 'seemingly constructed entirely out of cooling ducts'

# BMW M1

*BMW'S ONE AND ONLY MID-ENGINED SUPERCAR (SO FAR) WAS AN ABSOLUTE CRACKER*

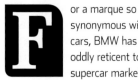

For a marque so synonymous with fast cars, BMW has been oddly reticent to enter the supercar market. With one wonderful exception...

It might be over 30 years old, but BMW's so-far only mid-engined car isn't embarrassed by more modern machinery, and neither is it the handful its advancing years might suggest. True, a peak output of 277bhp seems a bit sad next to, say, the E92 M3's 414bhp, but then, being plastic-bodied, it weighs just 1300 kilos whereas the M3 registers a rather more bulky 1580kg. All right, the M3 would pull away on anything resembling a straight but, when it was new, the M1 could hit 60mph from rest in 5.8sec and power on to an unrestricted top speed of 161mph.

And as we found out when we got all the M cars together in 2007, the M1 could stay in touch with the swiftest of the new bunch without the need for Chuck Yeager levels of bravery or standby underwear.

For an oldie, the M1 was remarkably easy to drive fast, reasonably civilised and amazingly user-friendly. It instantly felt special in the way only a genuine supercar can – hip-high roof, shallow nose, pop-up headlights, malevolently throaty exhaust note – and not because its acceleration was going to tear anyone's head off, though it's interesting to speculate just how close it might have come to achieving that in full, turbocharged race tune with 700bhp.

For raw, all-senses-engaged involvement, the M1 was something of a marvel, and if you did happen to find yourself with an armful of opposite lock half way round a glistening mountain hairpin, you wouldn't get bitten. Scalpel-like precision can never have been part of the design brief, but once you'd taken up a little of the slack mentally and tuned into the sublime balance and poise of the chassis, a dynamic repertoire of rare brilliance was there for the taking.

**SPECIFICATION**

**Years made** 1978-1981
**Engine** 6-cyl in-line, 3453cc
**Max power** 277bhp @6500rpm
**Torque** 239lb ft @5000rpm
**0-60mph** 5.8sec
**Max speed** 161mph
**Price** £26,810 (new) c£150,000 (today)

**evo RATING**
★★★★½

Left: cockpit wasn't the most flamboyant, but it functioned beautifully, as you'd expect from BMW

# Bristol Fighter

## WITH A V10 AND A 210MPH TOP SPEED, THE FIGHTER WAS A DIFFERENT SORT OF BRISTOL

For decades, this very English marque had built quirky GTs for gentlemen. Then, right out of the blue, it decided to build a supercar. It was as unexpected as Cliff Richard releasing an album of drum and bass – and, perhaps predictably, it wasn't a runaway success.

After half a century of building essentially the same car – the body styles may have changed but the basic template was large, luxurious, mildly sporty long-distance tourer powered by venerable Chrysler V8 – the Fighter was Bristol's launchpad into the 21st Century. Modified Chrysler Viper 8-litre V10, two seats, gullwing doors, 0.28 drag coefficient, a claimed 210mph and 0-60mph in 4sec. Perhaps it was all too much for Bristol's small but loyal clientele.

Toby Silverton, the jet-spares millionaire who bought Bristol from Tony Crook in 1997, did so with a view to exploiting untapped potential. The merging of missions was manifested in the Fighter, which, according to Silverton, had the potential to be the sanest, most practical 200mph+ supercar ever made. True, that image was muddled somewhat with the announcement of the twin-turboed, 1012bhp, Fighter T with its even lower 0.27 Cd, and Veyron-vaporising claimed 270mph top speed. The regular, normally aspirated £229,000 Fighter (525bhp, or 550 if you were closing in on 200mph, thanks to a mild ram-supercharging effect) wasn't exactly slow. Laid-back yet seductively rapid, it was a beguiling alternative to the usual suspects.

Unfortunately for Silverton, there were precious few customers who shared his vision, the Fighter struggled to sell, and in 2011 Bristol Cars went into administration. The marque was eventually bought by the Kamcorp Group, who intend to relaunch the Bristol name on electric cars. Which is only slightly more bizarre than the notion of a Bristol supercar...

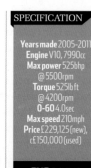

### SPECIFICATION

**Years made** 2005-2011
**Engine** V10, 7990cc
**Max power** 525bhp @5500rpm
**Torque** 525lb ft @4200rpm
**0-60** 4.0sec
**Max speed** 210mph
**Price** £229,125 (new), c£150,000 (used)

**evo RATING**
★★★★☆

Above: narrower, taller body than your average supercar had practical benefits. Right: Bristol adapted Viper V10 for Fighter

# Bugatti EB110 GT

## IT MAY NOT LOOK IT, BUT THE EB110 MIGHT JUST BE ONE OF THE ALL-TIME GREAT SUPERCARS

As the Veyron Super Sport does now, so in the early '90s the EB110 held the accolade of The World's Fastest Production Car. It was short-lived. The McLaren F1 arrived soon after and didn't so much move the supercar goalposts as uproot them and replant them, well, somewhere almost out of sight.

Such is life, but the EB110 – named to celebrate the 110th anniversary of Ettore Bugatti's birth – should be remembered for more than its brief spell at the top. It was very good – maybe too much so for its own good.

Like the Veyron, there was a 'hot' version, also named Super Sport. Introduced in March '92, six months after the launch of the EB110 GT, it was faster, lighter and sportier. It retained the GT's four-wheel drive but swapped some aluminium panels for carbonfibre, and was powered by a more potent version

**SPECIFICATION**

**Years made** 1991-1995
**Engine** V12, 3500cc, quad-turbo
**Max power** 552bhp @8000rpm
**Torque** 451lb ft @3750rpm
**0-60mph** 3.4sec
**Max speed** 212mph
**Price** £285,500 new, c£350-500,000 today

**evo** RATING
★★★★★

of the quad-cam, 60-valve, quad-turbo 3.5-litre V12. With bigger injectors, an exhaust system with two fewer catalysts and a new ECU, power rose from 550bhp to 603bhp.

When evo's John Barker drove a pristine example back in 2005, he wrote of the exceptionally smooth mapping of its fiery V12 and the finely judged ride and handling compromise. He called it 'befuddlingly, remarkably, outstandingly good', and after half an hour behind the wheel, couldn't help wondering why the EB110 wasn't generally regarded as one of the world's finest cars.

It was the first production car with a carbonfibre superstructure and generally overengineered to a faintly absurd degree. But, for an Italian supercar, the EB110 was surprisingly lacking in passion. It was very quick but, being so competent, so refined, so easy to drive and so conservatively styled, it didn't stir the emotions like a Diablo or 512TR. The EB110 really was the supercar that was too good.

Left and opposite: EB110's styling lacked the passion and flair of its contemporaries, but it was almost always the better car

# Bugatti Veyron 16.4

## IN 2005, BUGATTI REINVENTED THE SUPERCAR WHEN IT LAUNCHED THE 1000BHP VEYRON

To understand the Veyron you had to experience it, because at its launch in 2005 it was a car that defied description. Gnarled supercar veterans struggled to get any kind of handle on its capabilities, leaving to the imagination the sense of shock and awe accelerating to 100mph in 5.8sec or travelling at 250mph might engender.

Simple multiplication seemed to work best for anyone who'd experienced the heavy-fisted accelerative thump of Mercedes' supercharged, 500bhp SL55 AMG. The Veyron weighed about the same but was twice as powerful. It had almost twice the torque, too. And it felt roughly twice as fast. Or twice as fast as the fastest car you'd ever need. A Veyron could crush an Enzo, or any other of its supercar rivals, without trying.

And if all that sounds wonderfully absurd, you're in the right ballpark. The Veyron has as many turbos as it

SPECIFICATION

**Years made** 2005-2010
**Engine** W16, 7993cc, quad-turbo
**Max power** 1000bhp @6000rpm
**Torque** 922lb ft @2200rpm
**0-60mph** 2.8sec
**Max speed** 253mph
**Price** c£925,000 (new), c£1million (used)

**evo** RATING
★★★★★

has driven wheels (four apiece), two clutches, a seven-speed gearbox and very conservative 1000bhp. It got to 60mph in the time it took its driver to gulp.

Perhaps the most extraordinary thing about the Veyron was that it made its performance as accessible and useable as an Audi R8's (even if the top speed did require a special key, different set of tyres and access to Europe's fastest proving ground). That's what swallowed all that development money and took the time.

Given that the McLaren F1's record top speed had stood for a decade, it was hard to envisage a rush to topple the Veyron. But instead of being a great big full stop, the Bugatti soon became a convenient benchmark for any manufacturer that thought it was hard enough to measure itself against. The 1000bhp+ club soon included the Koenigsegg Agera, 9ff GT9-R, Hennessey Venom, and SSC Ultimate Aero TT, which in 2007 claimed the top speed record for America. Bugatti's reply would need to be emphatic...

Above: there are now other 1000bhp road cars, but none has the depth of engineering of the utterly stupendous Veyron

5346 WWL 167

Veyron

# Bugatti Veyron Super Sport

It was perhaps predictable that Bugatti wouldn't allow the upstarts across the pond at SSC to hang onto the 'world's fastest road car' title for long, but none of us expected the 'super Veyron' to quite so comprehensively eclipse everything that had gone before.

At the famous VW test track of Ehra-Lessien, the Veyron Super Sport posted a two-way average of 268mph (it went 271mph in the quicker direction). It also posted a 0-186mph (300kph) time of just 14 seconds (to put that in perspective, a Porsche GT2 RS takes exactly twice as long).

Quite simply, there has never been a road car like it, and given that Ferrari, McLaren et al seem to have given up chasing top speeds in favour of downforce and track times, it must be doubtful that any genuine production car will ever top it.

**SPECIFICATION**

**Years made** 2010-
**Engine** W16, 7993cc, quad-turbo
**Max power** 1183bhp @6400rpm
**Torque** 1106lb ft @3000rpm
**0-60** 2.5sec
**Max speed** 268mph (258mph for customer cars)
**Price** c£2,000,000 (new)

**evo RATING**
★★★★★

No question, the heart of the Super Sport is its phenomenal, 8-litre, quad-turbo W16 engine. Changes compared with the 'regular' Veyron engine included new, larger turbochargers, freer-flowing inlet manifolds, remapped ECU and bigger charge-coolers. The results were just startling.

When Chris Harris drove it for evo, he described it thus. 'There's quite a lot of turbo lag in the Super Sort: you push the throttle pedal down and it takes a second for the turbos to spool up. This is never a problem, because even while they're doing it, the car still feels as fast as a 911 Turbo...

'Tellingly, when there are two people in an SS they talk liberally because the thing is so damn refined, but when the taps open, there is silence. You can't talk because your brain is trying to work out if you were propelled at the horizon, or if the horizon was just dragged onto your face. It's uncanny, ludicrous and, I think, completely addictive.'

Above: no fripperies here. Super Sport's cockpit is brutally functional. Left: badge adorns newly enlarged chargecooler

# Caparo T1

## FORMULA 1 LEVELS OF LIGHTNESS AND CORNERING POWER MAKE THE CAPARO T1 UNIQUE

The dream: to build the world's swiftest road-legal car. The car that could cover the distance between two points on road or track, through a combination of near paralysing acceleration, cornering and braking, faster than any other. It was called the Caparo T1 and, powered by a naturally-aspirated 3.5-litre V8 developing 575bhp, it boasted a power-to-weight ratio of 848bhp per ton (for reference,

a McLaren F1 has 560). According to its makers, it was the closest anyone was going to get to piloting a modern F1 car without being a team driver.

Caparo Vehicle Technologies is a UK-based company at the cutting edge of advanced materials and engineering for not only automotive applications but also the aerospace industry. The T1, the creation of two ex-McLaren engineers, was intended as a rolling showcase for Caparo's various areas of expertise.

**SPECIFICATION**

**Years made** 2007-
**Engine** V8, 3500cc
**Max power** 575bhp
@10,500rpm
**Torque** 310lb ft
@9000rpm
**0-60mph** 2.5sec
**Max speed** 200mph+
**Price** £301,975 new,
c£250-280,000 used

**evo RATING**
★★★★½

On paper, the performance claims looked outrageous: 0-60mph in 2.5sec, 0-100mph in 4.9sec, 0-100-0 in 8.5sec, 3G cornering, 3G braking. The key element was lightness – the T1's kerb weight was about a third that of an average family saloon. The V8 engine – a joint development between Caparo and Menard Engineering – developed its 575bhp at 10,500rpm. Drive was directed to the rear wheels through a close-ratio sequential six-speed 'box made from magnesium and carbonfibre.

The T1 had its teething problems: it tried to set fire to Jason Plato and Clarkson declared it undriveable, which may have contributed to the fact that only around 20 have been sold. When evo tested it, we couldn't match the performance claims, though 0-60 in 3.8sec and 0-100 in 6.2 is hardly shabby, but it's the fastest road car ever on our test circuit. The T1 had fulfilled its remit and remains the most extreme and extraordinary car ever to wear a number-plate.

Left: smoke without fire. On this occasion the T1's only burning rubber; in an earlier test it had lightly singed Jason Plato

# Chevrolet Corvette ZR1

## THE ZR1 HAS ALWAYS BEEN THE ULTIMATE VETTE, AND THIS ONE'S THE MOST POWERFUL YET

In Europe, the Chevrolet badge is these days affixed to Korean-built budget cars, but in the US it's still good old Chevy, and its flagship – just as it has been since the '50s – is the Corvette. Now in its sixth generation, the Vette isn't the most sophisticated of beasts, but in ZR1 form it boasts genuine supercar performance.

Back in 2009, the peak power figure of 638bhp was pretty eye-widening, but it was the ZR1's torque that dried the mouth – 603lb ft, and all of it available at 3800rpm. Fortunately, the wheels hid huge carbon-ceramic discs, while weight was kept down to 1528kg by using carbonfibre for the roof, bonnet, splitter and front bumper. On paper, it all looked so promising, and at only a smidge over £100K, arguably the performance bargain of a generation.

And what an engine. A polycarbonate window in the bonnet-bulge revealed the aluminium top cover of a wide and

### SPECIFICATION

**Years made** 2009-
**Engine** V8, 6162cc, supercharged
**Max power** 638bhp @6500rpm
**Torque** 603lb ft @3800rpm
**0-60mph** 3.5sec
**Max speed** 205mph
**Price** £106,605 new, c£75-90,000 used

**evo** RATING
★★★★½☆

low, air-to-liquid intercooler. Below was an Eaton supercharger delivering up to 0.72bar of boost. The ZR1 had extraordinarily long intermediate gearing – with second good for 96mph and third for around 130(!) – but with so much torque it didn't really matter. Flatten the throttle and the fastest road-going Vette ever made hurled itself violently towards the horizon. Trouble was, the car appeared to grow around you like some Alice in Wonderland fairground ride, its

extremities becoming more and more remote. The Magnetic Selective Ride Control dampers sought to add a layer of chassis sophistication, but as evo's 2009 test showed, the Touring and Sport settings proved equally unsatisfactory, rendering the suspension either under-damped or rock-hard... What's more, on gargantuan tyres, it tugged, weaved and tramlined all at once. What the ZR1's claimed 7min 27sec lap of the Ring must have been like is unthinkable...

Opposite: ZR1 at the Nürburgring, where it lapped the notorious Nordschleife in a remarkable 7.27

# Chrysler Viper RT/10 & GTS

## *CONCEIVED AS A MODERN COBRA, THE VIPER AND ITS COUPE SIBLING WERE SUITABLY BRUTAL*

Chrysler may not have much of a name among fast cars fans, especially in Europe, but back in the late '80s Bob Lutz, one of the great enthusiasts of the motor industry, was its president, and it was Lutz who suggested that the Dodge division should consider making a modern-day Cobra.

The resulting Viper convertible was powered by an 8-litre V10 lifted from a truck (but fettled by Lamborghini) and it looked, well, every inch as venomous as its name. America took it to its bosom, only to discover it really did bite, as one high-profile customer – Kelsey Grammer of 'Frasier' fame – discovered when he rolled his.

The Viper didn't make it across the Pond until 1996, and we were a little slower to warm to its charms. Truth was, the RT/10 was tail-snappy and had a tent-pole roof that, when removed from the car, looked like a crashed hang-

### SPECIFICATION

**Years made** 1993-2010
**Engine** V10, 7997cc
**Max power** 400bhp @ 4600rpm (first gen)
**Torque** 450lb ft @ 3600rpm
**0-60mph** 4.6sec
**Max speed** 164mph
**Price** £55,000 new, c£15-40,000 used

### **evo** RATING
★★★☆☆

glider. April 1997 saw the launch of the more desirable GTS coupe version (now wearing a Chrysler badge) and this was much more like it.

Even better looking, it ran a lighter and modified V10 and had some aluminium suspension components. Still not the last word in handling finesse, it was a far better resolved car than the roadster and went on to spawn the rather excellent GTS-R Le Mans replicas in 1998.

Some loved the raw, earthy honesty of it all, others felt the Viper crude and uncouth. In 2003, it evolved into the SRT-10, which was more like a Corvette tribute act than the wild and, with a degree of rose-tinted hindsight, rather wonderful original. After production ended in 2010 it looked like that was the end of the story, but Chrysler has revealed a new Viper for 2013, with power up to 640bhp from an 8.4-litre V10. Whether it can recapture the feelings of awe inspired by the original, we'll have to wait and see.

Left: GTS version was lighter, faster and better than the original Viper. Hard not to love a car with an 8-litre V10

# Cizeta V16T

## THE EXTRAORDINARY V16-ENGINED CIZETA WAS THE VERY EMBODIMENT OF 1980s EXCESS

When wealthy businessman Claudio Zampolli, whose day job was selling and servicing Italian exotica in LA, got together with music composer/producer car nut Giorgio Moroder and ex-Lamborghini styling god Marcello Gandini to show the folk at Maranello and Sant'Agata how it was done, there wasn't much in the way of holding back. With the help of a group of ex-Lamborghini employees, they created a modest monster of a supercar called the Cizeta-Moroder V16T.

That the Cizeta had a 6.0-litre V16 engine was gobsmacking enough, but mounting it transversely made it one of the widest cars ever produced. The engine was actually two flat-plane V8s sharing a single block, the longitudinal transmission taking its input from the middle of the engine in a 'T' configuration. The motor was quite something, though, delivering its 560bhp

**SPECIFICATION**

**Years made** 1991-1995
**Engine** V16, 5995cc
**Max power** 560bhp
@8000rpm
**Torque** 469lb ft
@6000rpm
**0-60mph** 4.4sec
**Max speed** 204mph
**Price** c£200,000 new,
c£200-300,000 today

**evo** RATING
★★★★☆

at 8000rpm. Cizeta claimed 4.4sec to 60mph and a top speed of 204mph. And for anyone who'd ever wondered what 16 cylinders, four camshafts and 64 valves might sound like at full noise, the Cizeta provided the answer: simply awesome.

Why did it look so much like a Diablo? Because it was pretty much Gandini's original design for that car. And it's how the Diablo would have looked had it not been 'modified' by another design team when Chrysler took control

of Lamborghini in 1987. More than a little miffed by this, Marcello saw an opportunity to give the world his Diablo 'director's cut' with the Cizeta.

Although nine Cizetas were made, the company's viability looked increasingly suspect, all the more so when a frustrated Moroder and his money walked away, causing production to cease in 1995. Zampolli revived the design with a roadster in 2005 and promised more would follow. Little has been heard since.

Right: monster V16 sat transversely, which is what gave the Cizeta its colossal width. Styling was by Marcello Gandini

# Dauer 962 LM

## LOTS OF CARS PRETEND TO BE ROAD-RACERS. THE DAUER 962 LE MANS WAS THE REAL THING

**I**f you're going to modify a racing car design for the road, then it makes sense to modify one that raced on public roads. And if you're going down that path, it probably makes sense to choose, as your subject, the greatest car ever to score back-to-back wins in the world's greatest motor race that, in part, uses public roads. Which narrows things down a bit.

So perhaps it's no surprise that, back in the late '80s and early '90s, the sights and sounds of the Le Mans 24Hrs were no longer restricted to a small town in France over a weekend in June. Road versions of Porsche's legendary 962 were wearing number-plates and, if you were lucky, snorting and rumbling down a street near you.

A number of outfits tried their hand at the 962. Vern Schuppan's was pretty good, and there were also more than passable efforts from Koenig (the C62)

SPECIFICATION

**Years made** 1993-1995
**Engine** Flat-six, 2994cc, twin turbochargers
**Max power** 730bhp @7400rpm
**Torque** 517lb ft @5000rpm
**0-60mph** 2.8sec
**Max speed** 238mph
**Price** c£700,000 new, c£500K-£1million today

**evo** RATING
★★★★☆

and DP Motorsports (the DP 962). Eclipsing them all, however, was the Dauer 962 Le Mans created by ex-racer and team owner Jochen Dauer. It was so good, in fact, that Porsche teamed up with Dauer in 1994 and won Le Mans all over again.

Dauer's mission wasn't to produce a sanitised, road-legal facsimile of the Le Mans winner but actually improve it in the process. Although the starting point was a genuine 962 chassis, Dauer clothed it in a carbonfibre/Kevlar bodyshell and tweaked the aero too. Of its early-'90s contemporaries only the McLaren F1 would have been able to give the Dauer a hard time, and then only in a straight line. Mechanically, the Dauer differed from the 962 only in that it was more powerful. Divested of the need to comply with race regs, its mid-mounted twin-turbo 3.0-litre flat-six developed 730bhp. Just over a dozen Dauer 962s were built. Fortunately for today's hypercar owners, they're a very rare sight.

Left: cockpit was snug for two but sumptuously trimmed. In the mid-1990s nothing was quicker than a Dauer

# De Tomaso Pantera

## IN THE '70s, DE TOMASO WAS A MAJOR SUPERCAR PLAYER, THANKS TO A DEAL WITH FORD

Alejandro De Tomaso's Ford V8-powered supercar may have lacked the breeding of its Modenese contemporaries from Ferrari, Lamborghini and Maserati, but it never wanted for visual or aural drama. Firing up the GT5 version would have the windows of nearby houses rattling in their frames and teacups dancing on their saucers. The Pantera's 5.8-litre V8 didn't so much start as cough thunder.

The Pantera (Panther) was conceived as an image-boosting exercise for Ford in the early 1970s, filling the glamour vacuum left by the Le Mans-winning GT40. For the sake of expediency, its development was outsourced to De Tomaso in Italy. Ford engines were a given, of course, the 5.8-litre V8 supplying 330bhp and plenty of low-down torque through a ZF five-speeder.

A prototype (called simply the 351) was shown at the 1970 New York

### SPECIFICATION

**Years made** 1971-1992
**Engine** V8, 5763cc
**Max power** 350bhp
@5400rpm (GT5)
**Torque** 380lb ft
@3400rpm
**0-60mph** 5.4sec
**Max speed** 165mph
**Price** £41,000 new,
c£60-80,000 today

### evo RATING
★★★★☆

Show. Styled by Ghia's Tom Tjaarda, with chassis development carried out by ex-Lamborghini engineer Gianpaolo Dallara, the design was well received and showed great promise. With the longitudinally-installed V8 sitting ahead of the rear axle, it presented the intriguing prospect of being a major-league exotic – with all the style, performance and drama of its Italian contemporaries – but without the highly-strung temperament.

The Pantera went on sale in 1971. Unhappily, early cars were poorly made and unreliable. Elvis Presley is rumoured to have shot his after it refused to start. Despite growing acclaim for the way the car performed and handled (especially the 350bhp GTS version), Ford decided to cut its losses and stopped importing Panteras in 1975. De Tomaso moved to smaller premises in Modena and the Pantera remained largely unchanged for most of the next decade, a late evolutionary spurt coming in 1982 with the GT5 series, the last of which was sold in 1992.

Pantera lost some of its chiselled good looks as the years passed, though the late 'GT5' series of cars drove well

# Ferrari 365 GTB/4 Daytona

## FERRARI'S FIRST SUPERCAR WAS A 170MPH GT THAT COULD CRUISE ACROSS CONTINENTS

The Daytona was the fastest production car of its day, and not by a little but by a lot. Some tests put its top speed as high as 176mph and its 0-100mph time as low as 12.4sec. It had it all: dazzling speed, an impossibly long bonnet and monumental V12 power.

A counter to Lamborghini's Miura, the Daytona is now widely viewed as Ferrari's first supercar. In fact its official Ferrari name was 365 GTB/4 (it was dubbed Daytona by the press in honour of Ferrari's 1-2-3 in the 1967 Daytona 24 Hours with the 330P4).

The car's gifts to feeble, apprehensive flesh were profound and memorable: the dub-bass exhaust overlayed with quad-cam-drive shriek, the sharp metal clack of the open-gate gearchange, the rupture-weight clutch, the neck-bending acceleration. All of it was straight out of the supercar bumper annual. And all so achingly Italian.

True, the big front-engined GT was never just about straight-line performance. It promised to handle well for such a heavy car, partly because of the near equal front/rear weight distribution afforded by its five-speed transaxle. The cast alloy wheels, inspired by Ferrari's F1 cars of the day, looked serious, too. They were centre-locked onto splined axles. But the unassisted worm-and-peg steering was very heavy. Getting the car to change direction at all

### SPECIFICATION

**Years made** 1968-1973
**Engine** V12, 4390cc
**Max power** 353bhp @7500rpm
**Torque** 318lb ft @5500rpm
**0-60mph** 5.6sec
**Max speed** 176mph
**Price** £9927 new, c£220-320,000 today

**evo** RATING
★★★★☆

was an act of willpower. And using the ample muscle of the engine to drift the tail wide bordered on the foolish. That's why you'll hardly ever see a picture of the Daytona being driven sideways.

It was best to get it pointing in the direction you wanted to go, then open the taps. Deep down, the Daytona felt well sorted, but it steered like a truck, and was almost as heavy. As a trans-continental cruiser it was crushing; as an all-round supercar it was hard work.

First Daytonas had their headlights under perspex covers, but the US legislators insisted on these pop-up lights instead

# Ferrari 365/512 Berlinetta Boxer

## FERRARI FINALLY ACCEPTED ITS FASTEST SHOULD BE MID-ENGINED. THIS WAS THE RESULT

I t's a cast iron certainty that Enzo Ferrari didn't like taking a lead from Ferruccio Lamborghini but the Miura was stealing his thunder and there had to be a response. It was called the Berlinetta Boxer.

A mid-engined senior league supercar certainly wasn't a leap in the dark for Ferrari. It had its experience with the Dino to draw on and, of course, a wealth of know-how in F1 and sportscar racing.

Although lacking the sensual beauty of the Miura, Pininfarina designed a pretty and expertly proportioned body for the 365 Boxer, helped by the fact that although its 4.4-litre engine had 12 cylinders, they were in a flattened V with the opposing banks of cylinders set at a 180-degree angle rather than the more usual 90-degree configuration. This allowed a relatively low engine deck, despite the fact the 'flat'-12 sat above the five-speed transmission.

### SPECIFICATION

**Years made** 1973-1985
**Engine** Flat-12, 4390cc (365)
**Max power** 360bhp @7500rpm
**Torque** 333lb ft @4300rpm
**0-60mph** 5.7sec
**Max speed** 176mph
**Price** c£30,000 new, c£60-£130,000 today

**evo** RATING
★★★☆☆

The motor itself was clearly derived from the 3-litre powerplants used so successfully in the 312 B and B2 Grand Prix cars raced by the Scuderia between 1970 and '74. With four triple-choke downdraught Weber carburettors, it developed 360bhp at 7500rpm, enough to give the 1500-kilo BB a top speed of 176mph. The Bosch K-Jetronic fuel-injected BB512i introduced in 1981 was slightly quicker but even more driveable with, for the day, extraordinary engine flexibility. (Confusingly, 512 referred to the 5-litre flat-12 engine, when 365 came from the swept volume of one cylinder.)

The Boxer was a lovely thing to behold – a wonderfully understated counterpoint to the stylistic braggadocio of its rival, the Lamborghini Countach. It had a classic cabin, too. And a fabulously smooth engine with a broad powerband. But as a steer it was let down by a chassis that never really felt planted and was prone to serious lift-off oversteer. Dynamically, it was no match for the Countach.

Above: flat-12 gave the Boxer its name, but because it was positioned above the transmission, it also gave it serious handling issues

# Ferrari Testarossa/512TR/F512 M

## THE TESTAROSSA AND ITS DERIVATIVES WERE FERRARI'S FLAG-BEARERS RIGHT INTO THE '90s

**S**uccessor to the Berlinetta Boxer and destined to be locked in a desperate psychological arm-wrestle with Lamborghini's Countach, the Testarossa offered a crucial contrast in style and impact. Whereas the Lambo used its sharp angles and aggressive appendages for visual drama, the Ferrari relied more on its considerable width (it had 8cm on the Countach, itself hardly snake-hipped) and accentuated this advantage with flared slats and a shallow rear aspect. The overall effect was more conventional but combined a degree of subtlety with sledgehammer presence.

The Testarossa's 390bhp 4.9-litre flat-12 – toting just as many camshafts and valves as the Countach QV's V12 – was pretty much smashed to the table in the arm wrestle but was smooth, flexible and almost symphonically tuneful, sounding a bit like two Porsche 911s yoked together but with a very strong sense of 'stereo'. In truth, the Testarossa was a more softly focused machine than the Lambo – a superfast, two-seater GT rather than a raw, red-blooded racer.

But if the Countach was comfortably more accelerative, it was a closer run thing on top speed and the Ferrari had superior cruising refinement. For pure driving excitement, it had to be the Lambo, but the Testarossa was easier on the nerves and its flat-12 a great engine to live with.

It would undergo two major repackaging exercises – first in 1992 when it reappeared as the 512TR with a 428bhp version of the flat-12 and improved dynamics, and finally in 1994 as the F512 M, the M standing for the Italian *modificato*. The 440bhp 196mph F512 M was to be the last of the flat-12-engined Ferraris, truly the end of an era. The marque's next 'mainstream' supercar with a 12-cylinder engine would be the front-engined 550 Maranello.

### SPECIFICATION

| | |
|---|---|
| **Years made** | 1984-1991 |
| **Engine** | Flat-12, 4943cc (Testarossa) |
| **Max power** | 390bhp @6300rpm |
| **Torque** | 361lb ft @4500rpm |
| **0-60mph** | 5.2sec |
| **Max speed** | 178mph |
| **Price** | £63,000 new, c£50-100,000 today |

**evo** RATING
★★★★☆

Left: final F512 M version was better to drive than the early cars but a lot fussier in appearance too: check out the alloys

# Ferrari 288 GTO

## QUITE SIMPLY ONE OF THE FINEST – AND MOST BEAUTIFUL – SUPERCARS EVER CREATED

Strange, this. Wasn't the GTO just a 308 (very pretty, admittedly) with a few extra curves and slats? In part, yes. And the twin-turbo V8 that would go on to become the heart of the F40, of course. But there was something about the 1984 GTO that seems to transcend even this. It was just so devastatingly good looking – right up there with the Lamborghini Miura in the all-time drool parade.

Serious kit, too, with a composite body and longitudinal rather than transverse drivetrain. And what an engine. Saddled up with a brace of IHI turbos, the 2.8-litre V8 developed a phenomenal 400bhp (or 140bhp/litre) – enough, before the Porsche 959 came along, to make the 189mph GTO the fastest production car in the world. Not as hardcore as the subsequent F40 but none the worse for that; indeed many rate it as the better all-round steer (and it's much rarer too).

### SPECIFICATION

**Years made** 1984-1985
**Engine** V8, 2855cc, twin turbochargers
**Max power** 400bhp @7000rpm
**Torque** 366lb ft @3800rpm
**0-60mph** 4.9sec
**Max speed** 189mph
**Price** £72,999 new, c£400-600,000 today

**evo** RATING
★★★★★

Above: unlike its 308 and 328 siblings, the 288 had its V8 placed longitudinally, which necessitated a longer wheelbase

Short for Gran Turismo Omologato ('omologato' being Italian for 'homologated'), the three letters had appeared on a Ferrari once before, on a model considered by many to be one of the greatest Ferraris of all time: the 250 GTO. The new GTO clearly had a lot to live up to.

Crucially, unlike the 308, the GTO wasn't a semi-monocoque design but instead had a separate body over a high-tensile tubular-steel chassis. For strength and lightness, the bulkhead and front bonnet were made from a Kevlar glassfibre honeycomb composite, as used on Ferrari's F1 cars.

In 'Evoluzione' race-spec it could lay claim to 650bhp and, depending on gearing, a top speed of 225mph.

Rule changes meant the GTO never had a chance to prove itself in competition, but it didn't need to. Its performance, rarity and beauty, perhaps with a little help from the three letters on its rear, meant iconic status was assured.

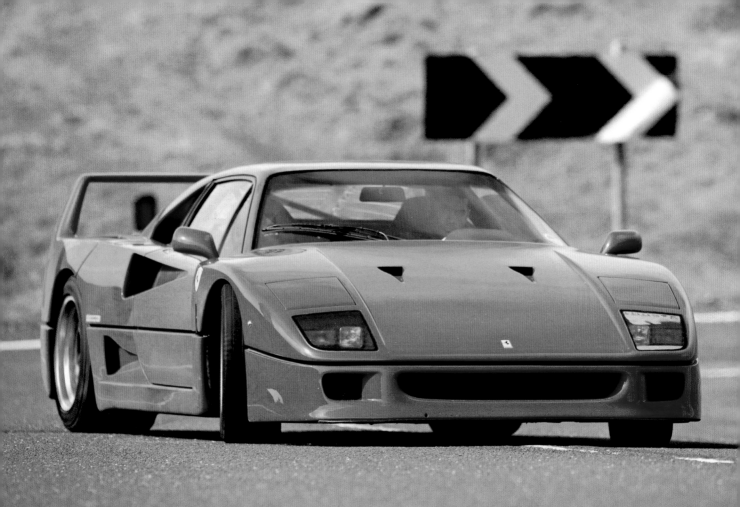

# Ferrari F40

## FERRARI TOOK EVERYTHING IT HAD LEARNED ON ROAD AND TRACK AND PUT IT INTO THIS CAR

It isn't hard to argue that the F40 is the greatest roadgoing Ferrari of all. The most exciting, the most focused, the most rewarding. In some ways, the shape said it all: fabulously functional and shorn of pretty much everything that didn't add to its speed and dynamic acuity.

Ferrari threw together the F40 in 12 months. Officially, it was to commemorate the company's 40th birthday in 1987, but everyone knew it was really revenge for Porsche's audacious act of one-upmanship with the 959. The F40's mid-mounted twin-turbo 2.9-litre V8 developed 478bhp. With a power-to-weight ratio of 441bhp-per-ton and almost 911-compact dimensions, its fusion of speed and size made the new Porsche supercar look vaguely unresolved. The 959 did sixty in about four seconds, the F40 went comfortably under; the 959 wouldn't quite do 200mph, the F40 did 201mph.

And, of course, the lean 1100-kilo kerb-weight had more than a little to do with it. So a tubular spaceframe, yes, but clothed in carbonfibre and Kevlar – perhaps the earliest manifestations of true F1 transfer.

Few supercars at the time – including even the McLaren F1 – felt as fast as the F40. It had something to do with how violently the turbos suddenly ramped-up the power. There was an intensity about the way the F40 accelerated that caught the breath every time. And could

seem overwhelming. Yet it wasn't. The compass of the chassis coped, however white-knuckled your wheelmanship. It was the fabulous steering, the tremendous grip, the blackout brakes, the surprisingly progressive breakaway...

The F40 cost more than twice as much as a Testarossa and, originally, Ferrari had intended to make just 450, but worldwide demand was so strong, production eventually hit 1311 in 1992 when Maranello finally called 'time'.

Lift the lightweight, carbon composite rear shell and there's no question that the F40 is as much race-car as road car

R181 LPD

# Ferrari F50

## THE F40'S REPLACEMENT WAS DISMISSED BY SOME AS A POSER'S SUPERCAR. BIG MISTAKE...

Ferrari's stated aim with the F50 was to deliver 'the emotion' of Formula 1 on the road. It had over 500bhp yet weighed just 1200kg. No traction control, no power steering, no anti-lock brakes. It was Ferrari's first fully carbonfibre monocoque road car and featured inboard, pushrod-operated suspension and that fabulous 513bhp 5.0-litre V12, mid-mounted and bolted to the tub.

The world had already marvelled at a not-dissimilar concept a year earlier in 1994 when McLaren launched the F1 and instantly established many new supercar benchmarks. The F50, however, demonstrated a rather more red-in-tooth-and-claw take on the idea.

Its engine was derived from the naturally-aspirated F1 3.5-litre V12 that Ferrari had designed to suit the new regulations at the end of the turbo era in 1989. As in the F1 car, this much-reworked and (to a degree) civilised engine was a structural, load-bearing component. You certainly knew you were sitting in a tub that was fixed to the engine, thanks to the commotion as the four-cam, 60-valve V12 climbed the lower slope of its torque curve, every shade of vibration discernable through the seat of your pants. Yet the ride was surprisingly supple, which added a compensating level of habitability.

Just about everywhere you looked in the simple cockpit was shiny carbonfibre

– even the gearknob was made from it – and the tub would tremble to the complex idle of the V12. The message coming through loud and clear was that this was one seriously focused Ferrari.

You had to work at it, take more notice of the feedback and get it to flow. But the satisfaction of driving it well was immense. It was all part of the unique experience the F50 delivered. Ferrari had produced a very worthy successor to its more lusted-after forebear.

Visually the F50 might have lacked the F40's focus, but when you drove it you knew this was a true hardcore Ferrari

# Ferrari Enzo

## THE ULTIMATE FERRARI ROAD CAR – SO FAR – AND ARGUABLY THE GREATEST SUPERCAR YET

The car most were expecting to be called the F60 arrived in 2002 and used a body of questionable beauty to generate increasing amounts of downforce with speed. Its construction combined carbonfibre and aluminium honeycomb throughout. The 6.0-litre V12 sitting in the middle was an all-new design, there was a paddle-shift gearchange, and the Enzo was also an early adopter of carbon-ceramic brakes.

Maranello's own description was 'the closest you can get to the F1 experience in a road car', which was at least a variation on its pitch for the F50. Naturally, this had more to do with the noise of the engine and the feel of the chassis than outright performance. Its naturally aspirated, 650bhp V12 screamed with the same nape-tingling intensity of the single seater's, even if its red line was set at a comparatively modest 8500rpm.

It was enough to convince you that

this was a far more serious attempt to recreate that Schumacher moment than even the F50. Everything, but everything, was designed to give the driver maximum input and gratification. The cabin was less spartan than the F50's but even more purposeful. The seats provided rock-solid location, the big high-tech instruments a truly epic rev-counter.

On a road that would make a 911 work for its living at 100mph, the Enzo tackled it at least 30 per cent faster without

breaking sweat, hitting absurd speeds on the shortest of straights. It might not have been quite as fast against the clock as a McLaren F1, but it was a lot more driveable. Anyone who climbed out of an Enzo and said it wasn't fast enough was either a liar or Michael Schumacher.

As a generator of thrills, the Enzo was phenomenal – the greatest ever Ferrari flagship without a doubt. Indeed, the Enzo was – arguably still is – the most exciting car on the planet.

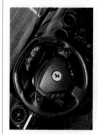

From its cockpit to its on-limit handling, the Enzo was all about providing the biggest thrill of any Ferrari yet built

# Ferrari 550 Maranello

*FERRARI RETURNED TO A FRONT-ENGINED LAYOUT FOR THE 550 MARANELLO. GOOD MOVE...*

Ferrari clearly used the Daytona as a spiritual template for the 550 Maranello. Both had bodies styled by Pininfarina with long, thrusting bonnets and short, clenched tails. Both had naturally aspirated front-mounted V12s powering the rear wheels via transaxle transmissions for optimum weight distribution. Both had big, clear rev-counters with red lines that began well beyond 7000. And both were set in the classic GT mould: large, leggy two-seater coupes that can traverse countries in a single bound.

But although the concepts overlapped, the scale of Ferrari's ambition had grown profoundly by the time it made the Maranello. Take the 550's V12 engine. It had 5.5 litres, 48 valves, 485bhp and 415lb ft of torque, its gearbox has six speeds (and 26mph/1000rpm gearing in top). The Daytona was the swiftest

**SPECIFICATION**

**Years made** 1997-2002
**Engine** V12, 5474cc
**Max power** 485bhp
@7000rpm
**Torque** 415lb ft
@5000rpm
**0-60mph** 4.3sec
**Max speed** 199mph
**Price** £143,680 new,
c£35-75,000 today

**evo** RATING
★★★★★

car of its day, but it was a pigmy next to the Maranello, which was 25mph faster flat-out and three seconds quicker to 100mph. Add to that a superbly positive gearchange, an almost absurdly driftable chassis and classy ergonomics. It was even refined.

The 575 that followed was faster still, but it needed the Fiorano handling pack to recapture the 550's brilliance. It might seem unsophisticated and lacking ultimate firepower compared with today's F12, but the 550 Maranello remains a dynamic masterpiece nonetheless.

Back in 2004, **evo** ran a 'Greatest Drivers' Car' showdown with the greatest cars from the previous ten years, including 911 GT3, Honda NSX-R and Zonda C12S. The 550 Maranello won. 'As with all great cars, there's no one facet that dominates the experience,' we concluded. 'Yes the engine is mighty, but the chassis is its equal. There's never been a supercar that's so exploitable and so rounded in its abilities.'

Left: earlier Ferraris had flawed, 'long-arms-short-legs' driving positions, but the 550 even had ergonomics sussed

# Ferrari 575M Maranello

*IT MAY HAVE BEEN FASTER THAN THE 550, BUT THE 575M TOOK A WHILE TO FIND ITS FEET*

Larger bonnet intake, reshaped front spoiler, xenon headlights and new five-spoke alloys – it took a real Ferrari fanatic to spot the visual changes when 550 Maranello morphed into 575M in 2002. The changes under the skin were more significant, the V12 engine enlarged from 5.5 to 5.7 litres, power pumped up from 485 to 508bhp, 0-60 cut from 4.3 to 4.1sec, and the official top speed just nudging past the 200mph barrier. Biggest change of all was the option of Ferrari's F1 paddle-shift transmission, which had first been seen on the 360 Modena F1.

The paddles seemed slightly out of keeping in a deep-lunged super-GT, the gearchanges not as smooth as they might be. No such misgivings about that magnificent V12 engine, which easily trumped the 550's already mighty delivery. The chassis lacked tight body control on challenging roads, however,

The early 575M had slightly disappointing handling, but once Ferrari introduced the Fiorano handling pack, it was sublime

and overall the 575 was viewed as a less satisfying car than the 550. Ferrari itself seemed to acknowledge the criticism when it introduced the 'Fiorano' handling pack not long after the 575's launch. With lower, tauter suspension and sharper steering, it recaptured the 550's magic, with an extra layer of ferocity on top.

After driving a 575 Fiorano last year, **evo**'s tester said: 'The way you can dictate to the chassis without every bullying it is just mesmerising. I'm bewitched...'

# Specialist Car Insurance

Adrian Flux know how much you love your car, that's why we are dedicated to finding you a great policy tailored to your specific requirements and driving history. Call us today for a free, no obligation quote.

**ADRIAN FLUX**

# 0800 081 8989
# adrianflux.co.uk

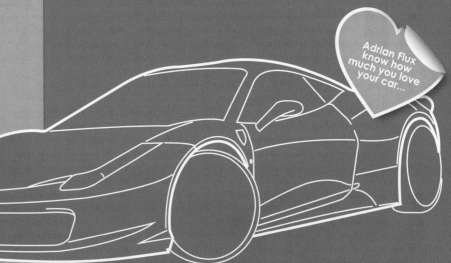

## High Performance Insurance

*Adrian Flux know how much you love your car...*

*Policy benefits can include:*

- EU Cover
- Track Day Cover
- Modified Cover
- Club Discounts
- FREE Legal Cover
- Limited Mileage Discounts
- European Breakdown Cover
- Advanced Driver Discounts

# Ferrari 599 GTB Fiorano

*FERRARI STUCK WITH FRONT-ENGINED FOR ITS NEXT SUPERCAR, AND WHAT AN ENGINE*

The V12 nestling well back in the long nose of the 599 GTB was derived from that of Ferrari's greatest supercar, the Enzo. The naturally aspirated 6-litre unit delivered a claimed 611bhp and 448lb ft, and having the engine set back behind the front wheels and the bulk of the car's other heavy components between the axles promoted an easy, natural handling balance. There was more.

The 599 also introduced such features as 'magnetorheological' semi-active dampers, a bespoke 'F1-Trac' dynamic stability system and the quickest-shifting version of the F1 auto-clutch manual yet, appropriately dubbed F1-SuperFast. The result was a car emphatically more advanced than the 550/575M it replaced.

It all worked superbly. On the road, the 599 was infused with a satisfying tautness. The transmission controlled the clutch more positively in manoeuvring

### SPECIFICATION

**Years made** 2006-2012
**Engine** V12, 5999cc
**Max power** 611bhp @7600rpm
**Torque** 448lb ft @5600rpm
**0-60mph** 3.5sec
**Max speed** 205mph
**Price** £212,066 new, c£80-£190,000 used

**evo RATING**
★★★★★

than other F1 types, but just as smoothly; the throttle and brake had good weight and feel. The V12 sounded glorious, and the ebb and flow of its complex, thunder-laden note when you pressed the throttle deeply in a high gear was epic. There was a distinct pick-up in the delivery at 3000rpm and another at 5500, by which time you were fast approaching three-figure speeds in fourth. The 599 merely felt like it was getting into its stride...

The contribution of the magnetic dampers went largely unnoticed – just as it should be. Roll, pitch and squat were tempered by the system, yet the 599 felt quite natural through a series of curves. Through the seat of your pants it felt like quite a heavy car, yet terrifically agile.

Meanwhile the F1-Trac system subtly modulated the power, based on the inputs of various sensors. Best of all, switch the manettino to its 'all off' setting and the 599 was easy to hold in a long, languid power-slide. To call it rewarding was an understatement.

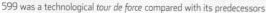

599 was a technological *tour de force* compared with its predecessors

# Ferrari 599 GTO

## FASTER THAN AN ENZO AROUND FERRARI'S TEST-TRACK, THE THIRD GTO IS ONE WILD RIDE

**F**errari trimmed around 100 kilos of excess fat from the 599 GTB Fiorano to create the 599 GTO – the third car from Maranello to wear the most celebrated set of initials in the history of fast cars.

The weight-shedding regime was fastidious. Forged wheels and titanium bolts saved 22kg, snug-fitting carbonfibre-shelled Sabalt seats trimmed a further 17kg, and on it went. With the output of the Enzo-derived V12 ramped up by 50bhp to a monumental 661bhp, the net effect was a power-to-weight ratio of 418bhp per ton, which put the GTO firmly amongst the world's most ferociously potent supercars.

According to Ferrari insiders, the GTO was deliberately set up like a racer to be unstable at the limits of grip – to make it more agile and more adjustable on the throttle. In other words, this was a car for serious driving enthusiasts, and at least as at home on a racetrack as on the public road. The GTB's sophisticated adaptive suspension was recalibrated, the wheels and tyres had grown, the brakes not only featured carbon-ceramic discs as standard but also carbon pads – a first on a road car. The upshot was that it was the fastest ever road car around Ferrari's own test track at Fiorano.

On the road, it made for a mind-expanding rush. The performance was other-worldly, the V12 sharp and angry in its upper reaches. Braking performance was absolutely mighty. The handling lived up to its promise: understeer had been banished, and if you were careless with brakes or throttle it could snap into oversteer.

The GTO was a proper, red-blooded Ferrari with a louder bark and a greater propensity to bite than the GTB; a wild ride but one just civilised enough to enjoy on the public road. It might not yet have the classic status of the two earlier GTOs but it's one very special Ferrari.

**SPECIFICATION**

**Years made** 2011-2012
**Engine** V12, 5999cc
**Max power** 661bhp @8250rpm
**Torque** 457lb ft @6500rpm
**0-60mph** 3.4sec
**Max speed** 208mph
**Price** £305,676 new, c£245-£320,000 used

**evo RATING**
★★★★★

Left: Enzo-derived 6-litre V12 was now producing an Enzo-trumping 661bhp in the GTO. Handling required skilled touch

# Ferrari FF

## THE FIRST EVER FOUR-WHEEL-DRIVE FERRARI IS ALSO THE WORLD'S HOTTEST HATCHBACK

A practical Ferrari sounds like a non sequitur, but with four seats, a hatchback coupe body and four-wheel drive – the first Ferrari so equipped – the FF certainly has the on-paper credentials. The question on most enthusiasts' lips was, could such a vehicle ever be a true Ferrari?

The four-wheel drive system works brilliantly, enabling the FF to deploy its 642bhp without drama – it simply fires out of corners with complete grip and maximum forward momentum. Its V12 engine, a new direct-injection unit different to the one in the 599 GTB, has a proper spine-tingling Maranello bark and is tuned to give its best right at the top of the rev-range. The carbon-ceramic brakes have that typically slightly grainy feel but deliver stupendous stopping power. The steering is as light and incredibly responsive as that of the mid-engined 458 Italia. The net effect is that although the FF feels like a big car when you first

Four-wheel drive gives FF stupendous cornering ability (top), while four proper seats (right) make it the Ferrari for families

### SPECIFICATION

**Years made** 2011-
**Engine** V12, 6262cc
**Max power** 642bhp @ 8000rpm
**Torque** 504lb ft @ 6000rpm
**0-60mph** 3.6sec
**Max speed** 208mph
**Price** £227,026 new, £180-200,000 used

**evo RATING**
★★★★★

climb in – and at just shy of five metres it's almost exactly the same length as an Audi A6 Avant – when you start really driving it seems to shrink around you.

In one way, all of this presents something of a conundrum. Because if you expect the FF to have a slightly more laidback persona, in keeping with its practical, GT-car appearance, such overt sportiness can be slightly jarring. But there can be no doubt at all that the FF is a proper Ferrari.

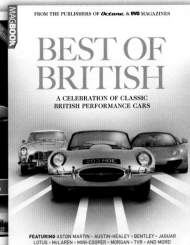
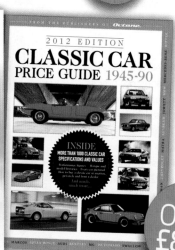

# Ferrari F12 Berlinetta

Ferrari's stated aim with the F12 was clear: to introduce mid-engined agility, traction and roll stiffness to the front-engined V12 range. In other words, make it handle like a 458 Italia. In the process, it has created a car that takes a giant stride over its 599 GTB predecessor – and indeed every other Ferrari that has gone before. With 730bhp, the F12 is the most powerful road car ever to wear that famous shield and the quickest around Fiorano, too. With a time of 1:23.0, it blitzes the hardcore 599 GTO by a full second and the Enzo by 1.9sec.

Switching back to a mid-engined configuration for the F12 was quickly dismissed – the benefits it brings in terms of centre-of-gravity and traction were outweighed by sacrifices to practicality, useability and visibility. The F12 had to retain the GT credentials revived by the 550 Maranello. So work began to create a lighter, lower, stiffer

Top: the F12's chassis balance is superb, initial understeer ebbing into a smidge of oversteer – or a whole heap of it if you ignore the warnings

structure with a weight distribution conducive to exceptional traction. The V12 is mounted further back in the chassis and 30mm lower, and the dash and seats are around 25mm lower, too. The overall weight distribution is 46:54, helped by the transaxle layout.

The 'aero bridge' in each front wing creates downforce by channelling air from the bonnet down the flanks. It also disrupts the wake from the wheel-wells to reduce drag. Ducts divert air from the rear wheelarches up through a grille on the fastback and onto the Kamm tail – in effect, a sort of 'blown' rear wing. In combination with a flat underbody and a substantial rear diffuser with four fins, downforce is increased by 76 per cent to 123kg at 124mph compared with the 599.

Remember the 599 carried those magnetorheological dampers? The ones with instantaneous response and unrivalled range? Well, the latest dual-coil piston reduces friction, has a wider force range and cuts overall response time by

# Ferrari F12 Berlinetta

75 per cent to just five milliseconds. Such is the pace of progress in Maranello these days. Then there's the seven-speed dual-clutch gearbox…

And at the heart of it all, the dry-sumped, direct-injection 6.3-litre V12, first seen in the FF, now produces 116bhp per litre and generates 80 per cent of its 509lb ft maximum torque from just 2500rpm. Prod the 'engine start' button on the tiny hexagonal steering wheel and it ignites instantly into a flat, busy idle.

Shortening the wheelbase and quickening the steering ratio was a key part of hitting those agility targets, but at first it makes the F12 feel darty and nervous, though you adjust to it. You also have to adjust to the almost overwhelmingly fierce acceleration that seems to grow in intensity with every engine revolution and every new gear. Then there's the way the rear of the car is so keen to point the nose into an apex, and the spikes of oversteer on the exit as you hit full throttle. That's not to say that the F12 is unpredictable or unmanageable, just that the scale of the performance, the speed you can carry and the neutral

balance demand that the driver stays completely focused on the job.

Turn off the electronic stability systems and the F12 doesn't fall apart or alter its essential character, doesn't suddenly become a mess of scrabbly wheelspin. In fact, once you adjust to that steering, the chassis balance is fantastically trustworthy, with mild understeer ebbing into a smidge of oversteer. You have to be quick to stay on top of the F12, but then you're going so fast that to expect

## SPECIFICATION

**Years made** 2012-
**Engine** V12, 6262cc
**Max power** 730bhp
@8250rpm
**Torque** 509lb ft
@6000rpm
**0-60mph** 3.0sec
**Max speed** 211mph
**Price** £239,736 new

**evo RATING**
★★★★★

anything else would be ridiculous.

The F12's vast performance gives it an edge over the 458 that never diminishes, even if it can't quite match the delicacy and control of the mid-engined machine. And while its wider role means it doesn't feel quite as focused as the 599 GTO, as a mad, life-affirming supercar, the F12 is pretty darn special. It also rediscovers the effortlessness that made the 550 and 575 so bewitching. Ferrari was right to stick with the front-engine layout.

# Car Insurance
## Be Wiser... Save Money

- The best policy at the best price
- Search over 30 insurers
- FREE RAC Breakdown

- FREE legal protection
- Instant cover and instalments
- Good credit rating? Save up to 40%!

**Freephone:**
# 0800 298 9649

**Online quotes at:**
# www.bewiser44.co.uk

# Be Wiser Insurance®

For all your insurance needs - car, motorbike, van, multi-vehicle, home & travel

# Ferrari 308/328

## THE 308 BEGAN A LINE OF V8-ENGINED FERRARIS THAT HAS LED ALL THE WAY TO THE 458

**T**he exquisite late-'60s Dino had introduced the idea of a 'junior' Ferrari. The next attempt to bring the prancing horse to the masses, the two-plus-two Bertone-styled Dino 308 GT4, had signally failed to live up to its gorgeous lines, but thankfully things were back on course when Ferrari revealed the two-seater replacement for the original Dino, the 308 GTB, in 1975.

Styled by Pininfarina – or more specifically Leonardo Fioravanti, who had also penned Daytona, Dino and Berlinetta Boxer – the 308 GTB (and its targa-top GTS sibling) was absolutely beautiful. Initially glassfibre-bodied, production switched to steel panels, which inevitably added some weight to the car, blunting the performance slightly. But it felt – and sounded – exotic enough.

To drive, it felt like a faster Dino, which was a good thing, and the 32-valve Quattrovalvole cars that followed felt fitter still. With no power steering and,

on the early cars, a heavy clutch, the 308 was quite physical to drive, especially at low speeds, and the dog-leg open-gate gearshift required some mastering. It wasn't all that fast – 0-60mph in 6.7sec for the 308 – but with a bevy of carbs gargling away and a throttle response sharp enough to splice a human hair, it pressed all the right Ferrari buttons.

For the 328 introduced ten years later, the engine's capacity was increased from 3.0 to 3.2 litres and power jumped to

270bhp, cutting the 0-60 time to 5.5sec and lifting the top speed to 166mph.

A piece of 328 trivia – from 1986 to 1989, Ferrari produced a 2-litre version with a turbocharged engine specifically for the Italian market where there were tax breaks for sub-2-litre cars.

Around 20,000 308s and 328s were made in total, and with secondhand values still hovering around the £30,000 mark, they represent a great entry point to classic Ferrari ownership.

## SPECIFICATION

**Years made**
1975-1985 (308),
1985-1989 (328)
**Engine** V8, 2927cc (308)
**Max power** 252bhp
@ 7700rpm
**Torque** 209lb ft
@ 5000rpm
**0-60mph** 6.7sec
**Max speed** 157mph
**Price** c£30,000 new,
£30-35,000 today

**evo** RATING
★★★★☆

252bhp isn't much these days, but with its carbs gargling and instant throttle response, 308 could still be intoxicating

# Ferrari 348/F355

## THE UNDERACHIEVING 348 MORPHED INTO THE SUPERB – AND UTTERLY GORGEOUS – F355

One of the most widely derided Ferraris is the 348, introduced in 1989. It quickly gained a reputation for edgy handling, while its chunky lines and Testarossa-style slatted side air-intakes compared unfavourably with the gorgeous 328 it had replaced.

In fact today the 348 is being reappraised, with much to enjoy in its V8 and unassisted steering, so long as you don't take too many liberties with the handling. But in the mid-1990s, Ferrari urgently needed a return to form, and the 355 that replaced the 348 in 1995 was just the car.

The 355 introduced five valves per cylinder to the stalwart V8 (that was the '5' in 355, creating yet another Ferrari naming system), not to mention dry-sump lubrication, titanium conrods and a six-speed gearbox.

The F355 was also significant for being the first Ferrari to be offered with the

### SPECIFICATION

| | |
|---|---|
| **Years made** | 1990-1994 (348), 1994-1999 (F355) |
| **Engine** | V8, 3496cc (F355) |
| **Max power** | 374bhp @8250rpm |
| **Torque** | 268lb ft @6000rpm |
| **0-60mph** | 4.7sec |
| **Max speed** | 183mph |
| **Price** | £83,031 new, £35-55,000 today (F355) |

**evo RATING**
★★★★☆

F1-derived paddle-controlled electronic gearshift system with its automated clutch. Meanwhile its revised suspension, with electronic dampers, cured the 348's worst tendencies. Arguably, never had so much Pininfarina beauty, scintillating V8 music and fine handling been poured into an entry-level Ferrari.

But then Ferrari's pride had been at stake, the 348 regularly bested by not only the contemporary Porsche 911s but also Honda's new NSX. The F355 had to be better than good, and it was.

Even today, it's the mid-engined Ferrari you'd probably buy if you couldn't stretch to a 458. It wouldn't be as fast, of course – 0-60mph in a claimed 4.7sec felt if anything a little on the optimistic side – but it would make you sigh with satisfaction just the same. With prices today starting at just a little over thirty grand, it's a hugely tempting secondhand buy. And the 348 can be had for even less, with even well-cared-for examples available for as little as £25K.

Above: 348 could be tricky at the limit. Right: look, no gearlever! F355 was first Ferrari to feature F1 automated 'box

# Ferrari 360 Modena/Challenge Stradale

## THE 360 WAS A BIG STEP ON FROM THE 355, CULMINATING WITH THE SCINTILLATING STRADALE

Tough act to follow, the F355. After all, it was such a pretty, finely-balanced thing. Could it be finessed? Probably, but Ferrari didn't want to run the risk of trying and failing. So its 1999 successor, the 360, wasn't as achingly lovely. It lacked something of the 355's sweet, tactile nature. Instead, Ferrari started again and set off in a different direction: more power, more noise, more resolve and, ultimately, more thrills.

With 394bhp on tap from a 3.6-litre V8, the 360 Modena had 20bhp more than the F355 and moved the game on with its innovative engineering solutions, not least in its aerodynamics and use of aluminium structures. F1 paddle-shift was again optioned as an alternative to the six-speed, open-gate manual and, in 2000, the fabric-roofed Spider appeared.

Both cars offered a step-change in practicality for entry-level mid-engined Ferraris. Promo videos had Eddie Irvine casually lobbing a bag of golf clubs into one. The doors opened wider, the sills were narrower.

The range was expanded again in 2003 with the arrival of the 360 Challenge Stradale – effectively a road-legal version of the Ferrari 360 Challenge race car. And suddenly the 360 became a whole lot more exciting. It might have been, in essence, a 360 with a loud exhaust, stripped-out cabin and stickier tyres, but the modifications unleashed the beast within. With power up to 420bhp and the 0-60 time down to 4.1sec, the Stradale felt like a different sort of Ferrari.

The extra noise, bite, response, grip and braking power – those ceramic stoppers were immense – made an already addictive driving experience completely intoxicating. The manic scream and shove of the flat-plane crank V8 struck a crucial difference. Blinding chassis, too. Driving the Challenge Stradale flat-out was an adrenalin rush like little else.

Not as pretty as a 355, but a thoroughly modern Ferrari. Right: an increasingly rare sighting of a lovely, open-gate manual 'box

| SPECIFICATION | |
|---|---|
| **Years made** | 1999-2004 |
| **Engine** | V8, 3586cc |
| **Max power** | 420bhp @8500rpm (CS) |
| **Torque** | 275lb ft @4750rpm (CS) |
| **0-60mph** | 4.1sec |
| **Max speed** | 186mph |
| **Price** | £133,025 new, £80-100,000 today (CS) |

**evo RATING**
★★★★★

# Ferrari F430/Scuderia

## FERRARI HIT A NEW HIGH WITH THE F430, ESPECIALLY IN TRACK-INSPIRED SCUDERIA GUISE

How about a car with an aura that makes the small hairs on the back of your neck stand up merely walking towards it? In 2007, Ferrari unveiled the 430 Scuderia, its boldest attempt yet to bring F1 technology and excitement to a road car. Former race boss Jean Todt had just become CEO of the car division too, so the transfer of ideas, technology and engineering from F1 to the road car programme – always present as a strong undercurrent at Maranello – had gained a new, arguably defining, impetus.

The Scuderia's power hike – up 20bhp on the already brilliant F430 – was perhaps as predictable as the 100 kilos sliced from the weight. But power-to-weight was just the starting point for the Scuderia. By combining the E-diff from the F430 and the 599 GTB's F1-trac traction control system, Ferrari had created possibly the ultimate high-performance driving aid. The system

allowed the rear diff and traction control to work in concert, feeding in precisely the right amount of torque for the swiftest exit from any bend, even with the throttle nailed to the carpet (if there was any). It trimmed entry-lines under braking, too. The Scuderia felt very different to the regular F430, not least the way, in a heartbeat, it could flip between mild-mannered docility and feral ferocity. It all pivoted around 3500rpm, at which point the exhaust valves opened

and the transmission shift program switched from easy-does-it to let-'em-have-it: 503bhp and 347lb ft spat at the tarmac in rapid-fire chunks of scalp-prickling fury just 60 millisecond apart.

The exhaust at full throttle was loud and penetrating enough to blow chunks off buildings. The steering was exceptionally direct and precise. What's more, you could 'over drive' it in the most outrageous manner and the chassis would look after you.

Left: compare the Scuderia's cockpit with earlier Ferraris, and the adoption of motorsport themes and tech is obvious

# Ferrari 458 Italia

## LATEST IN THE LINE OF V8 MID-ENGINED FERRARIS, THE 458 ITALIA WILL BLOW YOU AWAY

A s an automotive sculpture, the 458 Italia recalled Miura levels of beauty. But it was the kinetics that knocked us sideways. Designed to replace the F430 and Scuderia, it was a completely new car in all respects. Even the engine was new, a 4499cc V8, with a flat-plane crank and direct injection. It delivered 562bhp at a seemingly insane 9000rpm.

Helping translate its wild 384bhp-per-ton power-to-weight ratio into 0-60 in 3.4sec was Ferrari's sensationally swift seven-speed dual-clutch transmission. It was an F1 transfer showcase, too, with the latest generation E-Diff differential and F1-Trac skid control systems.

But even that gave scant notice of the way it would drive or how radical the new ergonomic regimes would seem from behind the wheel. The all-new dashboard design featured a trick TFT display alongside the dials to show how the different elements of the car were performing. Indicator and wiper stalks were absent, too, the functions moved to neat little buttons on the steering wheel.

No, the 458 wasn't the normal updated V8 berlinetta. It did things that other – perhaps lesser – machines could not. The steering was very fast and light, throttle response especially sharp. The performance was simply startling. It hauled from 2500rpm in one great wall of noise, and those seven ratios were so closely stacked – and the gearshift so fast – that the impression was of one long, sustained rush of acceleration.

You conduct the car with your wrists, making small, neat inputs. You lean on the systems to transfer as much of that 562bhp to the surface as possible and you almost forget about the gearshift because it's so damn efficient. You cover ground at an extraordinary rate, you grin at the arrogance of the engine and you admire – greatly admire – the technical omniscience of Ferrari's achievement.

Above: the 458's surfaces each have an aerodynamic function, but the combined effect is also one of jaw-slackening beauty

# Ford GT40

## WAS FORD'S GT40, RATHER THAN LAMBORGHINI'S MIURA, THE WORLD'S FIRST SUPERCAR?

**B**orn out of an almighty falling-out between Henry Ford II and Enzo Ferrari, the GT40 in its various guises won Le Mans four times between 1966 and 1969, and the roadgoing versions can lay serious claim to being the world's first supercars as we now understand the term.

Ford was determined to win Le Mans, and when a mooted takeover of Ferrari fell through, it turned to the British company Lola to develop a mid-engined Ford-powered endurance racer. There were several variations over the years, with engines ranging from 4.2 to a mighty 7 litres.

The MkIII version from 1969 pictured here, which John Simister drove for *evo*'s tenth birthday issue back in 2008, was the closest the GT40 came to being a genuinely useable road car, although it was still very much a racer at heart.

Even with its 5-litre V8 in a fairly mild state of tune, the MkIII is still a serious performance car. The ZF gearbox is co-operative, the twin-plate clutch properly progressive, the ride and noise levels just about acceptable for a drive down to Le Mans...

Squeeze the throttle hard and there's a bellow somewhere behind, the Ford squats its tail and leaps forward, accelerating hard well into three-figure speeds. Despite appearances, it's a small car, which makes it a terrific overtaker, with a sound barrage to stun all opposition. This road car had a top speed of around 165mph; the racers regularly broke 200mph on the Mulsanne straight. When John Simister drove the mkIII around the famous circuit, he found its handling first-rate, the steering quick and full of feedback, just as you'd hope.

Just 107 GT40s were produced and the originals – much copied – are among the world's most sought-after classics. Whether it was the first supercar is still debated, but what a machine.

**SPECIFICATION**

**Years made** 1964-1969
**Engine** V8, 4949cc (mk III)
**Max power** 306bhp @ 6000rpm
**Torque** 329lb ft @ 4200rpm
**0-60mph** 5.3sec
**Max speed** 165mph
**Price** £7549 new, c£1-3million today

**evo** RATING
★★★★★

Top: mkIII wasn't the prettiest GT40, but it was the closest to a genuine road car. Elongated tail was to provide a boot

DWC 8G

# Ford GT

So was the 1960s Ford GT40 the original supercar? Ford clearly thinks so. In 2004 it made good on its promise that the iconic old-timer would ride again by launching the Ford GT, a car with which to bait and beat Ferrari, just as the original had done all those years ago.

The Ford GT looked just like the '60s Le Mans legend it paid tribute to. That was important; shapes really didn't come much better. But it wasn't a replica, being bigger in every direction.

The entire body (save for the glassfibre engine cover) was made from lightweight aluminium and it clothed a substantial aluminium spaceframe structure, on which forged aluminium wishbones were hung at each corner.

Power came from a quad-cam 5.4-litre V8, supercharged to 550bhp with a colossal 500lb ft of torque. The power-to-weight ratio of 353bhp per ton was hardly less impressive. From rest to

100mph took just 7.8sec and the top speed was 205mph. A GT40 simply wouldn't have been able to keep up.

No doubt about it, the motor was a monster. Not sharply aggressive but progressive and linear, with an absolute wall of power from no revs to 6500rpm.

The gearing was extraordinary too, with second and third good for almost every situation. You could leave it in second on the exit of a 30mph limit, floor it and just a few seconds later be

doing over 80mph. If you wanted to savour the experience a little more, do the same thing in third and you'd slam up to 130mph and beyond before you needed another gear.

The chassis, meanwhile, felt so composed that you couldn't help but revel in its ability and security. Few of the GT's supercar contemporaries felt so devastatingly rapid and yet so unerringly friendly, and in 2005 the Ford beat all rivals to be **evo**'s Car of the Year.

## SPECIFICATION

**Years made** 2004-2006
**Engine** V8, 5409cc, supercharged
**Max power** 550bhp @6500rpm
**Torque** 500lb ft @3750rpm
**0-60mph** 3.7sec
**Max speed** 205mph
**Price** £120,900 new, c£120-150,000 today

**evo** RATING
★★★★★

Modern GT was a respectful homage to the '60s original, though bigger in every dimension. V8 was supercharged

# Gumpert Apollo S

## DEVASTATINGLY QUICK ON TRACK, THE APOLLO HAD ABILITY TO MATCH ITS BRUTAL LOOKS

The brainchild of former Audi engineer Roland Gumpert, who was based in Altenburg in the far east of Germany, the genesis of the Apollo leaned heavily on his racing experience and his enduring links with the Ingolstadt manufacturer.

Gumpert Sportwagenmanufacktur was established in 2004, and the first customer Apollo appeared the following year. Using a twin-turbocharged version of Audi's 4.2-litre 90-degree V8 – complete with lightweight internals – and mated to a six-speed sequential transmission, the Apollo was initially offered in three versions: the 690bhp S as tested by evo back in 2006, the 641bhp entry-level Apollo or the lighter and more powerful (789bhp) R. Even in S trim, it cost over a quarter of a million and promised a top speed of around 225mph, together with mind-altering race-car-for-the-road dynamics.

| SPECIFICATION | |
| --- | --- |
| Years made | 2005-2012 |
| Engine | V8, 4163cc, twin-turbo |
| Max power | 690bhp @6300rpm |
| Torque | 675lb ft @4000rpm |
| 0-60mph | 3.0sec |
| Max speed | 220mph+ |
| Price | £275,000 new, c£200,000 -£250,000 used |

### evo RATING
★★★★☆

It wasn't all whiz-bang, OMG acceleration, though. Belying its intimidating looks, the Apollo is an easy and undemanding car to guide at sane speeds, with steering that is both light and linear, the front end responding directly but with encouraging feel. Massive reserves of grip, yes, but it far from dominates the experience. The Apollo's chassis is talkative and reactive with the reassurance that the front tyres are the first to find their limit, the tail feeling supremely tied-down, even at the extremely elevated road speeds of which the Apollo is capable. On a track, it's just mighty. Around evo's test track the only supercars faster are the Caparo T1 and Ferrari 458 Italia.

In 2010, Gumpert announced plans to put a second model, the similarly rapid but more attractively styled Tornante, into production. Sadly Gumpert Sportwagenmanufacktur went into administration in 2012 and any further production is now in doubt.

Left: a clear case of form following function. Audi V8 had twin turbos and made 690bhp

# Hennessey Venom GT

*VEYRON POWER AND SPEED IN A MUTANT LOTUS BODYSHELL, THAT'S THE VENOM GT*

Texas-based Hennessey Performance has long been celebrated for extracting big power from American muscle-cars, but in the last few years it has also become famous for a Veyron-trumping Lotus-based supercar.

So ask yourself this question. What would a Lotus Exige be like if it had 1244bhp? Undriveable would be one answer. A crash looking for somewhere to happen might be another. But possibly, just possibly, the biggest thrill anyone has ever had at the wheel of a road car is the right one. That's what Hennessey believed, anyway, when they stretched and the baby Lotus to accommodate a massively uprated version of the 6.2-litre V8 from the Corvette ZR1. There are three states of tune. Merely 'very scary' gets you 725bhp, then there are two twin-turbo versions with either 1000bhp or the full OMG 1244bhp.

**SPECIFICATION**

**Years made** 2011-
**Engine** V8, 7000cc, twin-turbo
**Max power** 1244bhp @6500rpm
**Torque** 1155lb ft @4200rpm
**0-60mph** 2.5sec
**Max speed** 275mph
**Price** c£400,000

**evo** RATING
★★★★½

Oh, and the Venom GT weighs 1220kg, giving the 'full house' version a power-to-weight ratio of around 1000bhp-per-tonne. Hennessey claims a 0-200mph of 15.3sec, more than a second better than a Veyron's.

The team behind it are all steeped in motorsport, coming from Formula 1, Le Mans and Bonneville backgrounds. So it's no surprise to find that the Venom's bodywork and wheels are carbonfibre, that there's an adjustable rear wing, active aerodynamics and adjustable suspension, too. Tyres are Michelin Pilot Super Sports – a massive 345/30 on 20in rims at the rear. Discs are carbon-ceramic, gripped by Brembo six-piston calipers at all four corners.

Company boss John Hennessey describes the Venom GT as 'the supercar I have always dreamed of building'. Constructed in Britain, and with a chassis developed on our roads, the Venom GT might also just turn out to be the Veyron Super Sport driver's worst nightmare.

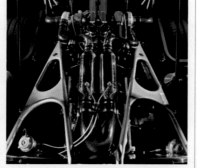

Under the stretched Exige skin is this monster twin-turbo V8. Opposite: new Roadster version

# Honda NSX/NSX-R

## THE NSX WAS A BIT TAME BY SUPERCAR STANDARDS; NOT SO THE TRACK-BRED NSX-R

It isn't that hard to understand why some felt unfulfilled by the NSX. For all its undoubted gifts, it always seemed essentially 'safe' rather than 'scary', always inspired enough confidence to be conducted at a considerable lick without putting undue pressure on the driver. Arguably, it was the world's first truly friendly supercar. Yet the fact is, as Honda eventually showed with the NSX-R, red-blooded

involvement and precision-guided technology weren't mutually exclusive. Mixed together in the right proportions they could deliver extraordinary results, whichever sort of driver you were.

A road-going racer designed to kick Skyline and Supra butt in Japan's JGTC race series, the NSX-R never officially made it to the UK, which was a tragedy. Lighter, harder, faster and hornier than the standard item, it would have been the perfect repost to the 911 GT3 and 360 CS.

### SPECIFICATION

**Years made**
1990-2005
**Engine** V6, 3179cc
**Max power** 276bhp
@ 7100rpm (NSX-R)
**Torque** 224lb ft
@ 5300rpm
**0-60mph** 4.4sec
**Max speed** 168mph
**Price** c£65,580 new (in
Japan), c£60,000 today

### evo RATING
★★★★★

It was also **evo** Car of the Year of 2002.

According to Honda, the quicker (4.4sec) 0-60mph time was purely due to the weight savings and slightly shorter gearing which, incidentally, knocked the top speed down to 168mph. The 3179cc V6 was rated at just 276bhp at 7100rpm with 224lb ft at 5300rpm. Our guess was a bit more. Certainly, the sharper throttle response and more 'urgent' feel suggested more gee-gees than Honda was prepared to admit to.

The NSX-R got the job done like no other sub-300bhp supercar on earth. Traction off the line was stunning, the rifle-bolt action of the six-speed 'box so fast and accurate you could dazzle yourself with your own hand speed. And what a noise: a howl so hard-edged it could chisel granite.

It's hard to recall steering that resolved information about the road surface more organically than that of the NSX-R. The confidence it gave was astonishing. Much like the car itself.

Regular NSX (above) was arguably the first truly useable supercar. NSX-R (opposite) was one of the greatest

# Jaguar XJ220

*VILIFIED AT BIRTH, JAGUAR'S XJ220 IS NOW RECOGNISED AS ONE OF THE SUPERCAR GREATS*

One of the most extraordinary and beautiful cars ever to reach production, the world's first hypercar (hitting close to 220mph while the McLaren F1 was still climbing off the drawing board) was vilified at its birth in 1992 for not having the 500bhp V12 engine, four-wheel drive and scissor doors promised in the concept and, at nearly 7ft wide, being too big for British roads.

That it ended up with an even more potent (542bhp) twin-turbo V6 and lighter, rear-drive powertrain didn't cut much ice back then, though ironically the approach would have garnered more acceptance now. The XJ220 was regarded as something of an over-sized freak, an outsider that was never invited to join the cosy supercar cabal.

The child of a collaboration between Jaguar's so-called 'Saturday Club' – an informal group of engineers, including

engineering chief Jim Randle, who'd get together after hours to develop pet projects – and Tom Walkinshaw's TWR Engineering, the genesis of the XJ220 formed around Randle's idea to make a lightweight, mid-engined two-seat Jaguar that would eclipse the Ferrari F40 and Porsche 959. In the event, only 281 XJ220s were made between 1992 and 1994 against a projected production run of 350. The motoring press loved it, but commercially the XJ220 was a fiasco.

A lot of the blame was laid at its Metro 6R4-derived V6 – and its sheer girth. True, there were things you had to adjust to in the XJ220 – size, turbo lag, steering that initially seemed heavy and unresponsive, strong understeer in the tightest bends, brakes that weren't really up to the job – but, learn its ways, and it was actually well poised, translating serious stonk into stunning speed across the ground through a polished fusion of grip, neutrality and benign adjustability. If only it hadn't been so wide.

## SPECIFICATION

**Years made** 1992-1994
**Engine** V6, 3498cc, twin-turbo
**Max power** 542bhp @7200rpm
**Torque** 475lb ft @4500rpm
**0-60mph** 3.7sec
**Max speed** 213mph
**Price** £430,000 new, c£150-£250,000 today

**evo RATING**
★★★★★

Above: still one of the most beautiful of all supercars, XJ220 was compromised by its powerful but rough-sounding V6

# Jaguar XJR-15

## THE 'OTHER' JAGUAR SUPERCAR WAS IN FACT A ONE-MAKE RACER ADAPTED FOR ROAD USE

If the term 'supercar' had been around in the 1950s, it might well have been applied to Jaguar's stupendous XKSS, essentially the Le Mans-winning D-type in roadgoing form. Jaguar produced many great sports cars over the years, of course, from XK120 to E-type to current XKR-S. But only two actual supercars have worn the Jaguar badge, and, by a slightly uncomfortable coincidence, they came out within months of each other...

Built specifically for a race series called the Intercontinental Challenge by Jaguar Sport, a subsidiary of Tom Walkinshaw Racing (TWR), the XJR-15 was essentially an XJR-8 Le Mans car with an all-new Peter Stevens-designed Kevlar and carbonfibre body. Unlike the turbo V6-engined XJ220, it was powered by a normally aspirated 6-litre V12 engine, developing 450bhp, and retained the race car's basic chassis layout. To many

enthusiasts, its taut, feline lines combined with the fact that it had a V12 engine made it an attractive alternative to the 'official' Jaguar supercar.

Weighing just 1050kg, the XJR-15 could sprint to 60mph in 3.9 seconds and was geared for a top speed of 191mph. In race trim, the full ground-effect body endowed it with very serious cornering pace. But as a road car the XJR-15 was unapologetically raw, hardly bothering to mask its competition roots.

For customers brave enough to want to use the car on the road, Jaguar Sport fitted bumpers, indicators and raised the overall ground clearance. Unfortunately, this had rather malign consequences for the handling as the undertray aerodynamics and suspension were optimised for the ground-skimming ride height. The result was a car that always felt on the edge of oversteer. And, when it came, it required very quick and accurate correction, or else. That Stevens-penned body *was* beautiful, mind.

Left and opposite: XJR-15 in livery for the Intercontinental Challenge race series for which it was originally intended

# Jaguar C-X75

## THE MOST RADICAL SUPERCAR YET SEEN WILL SOON BE A PRODUCTION REALITY

Jaguar has confirmed that its C-X75 plug-in hybrid supercar will definitely be going into production – and its technical specification is truly mind-boggling.

It will feature two high-powered axial-flux electric motors, one powering the front axle via a single-speed gearbox, the other powering the rears via the main seven-speed automated manual gearbox.

These powerplants are said by Jaguar to have three times the power density of conventional electric motors, and are supplemented by a high-tech 1.6-litre twin-charged (supercharged *and* turbocharged) four-cylinder petrol engine producing in excess of 500bhp at 10,000rpm. Think in terms of future Formula 1 engines...

The performance projections are off the scale. Jaguar says the C-X75 will hit 60mph in 3sec and 100mph in 6sec, comfortably topping 200mph.

The main body will be constructed

Above: we've only seen the C-X75 concept so far, but Jaguar says the production car will be equally stunning

## SPECIFICATION

**Years made** 2014-
**Engine** 4-cyl petrol plus two electric motors
**Max power** 500bhp-plus
**Torque** n/a
**0-60mph** 3.0sec
**Max speed** 205mph
**Price** c£800,000

**evo** RATING
★★★★★

entirely from carbonfibre with aluminium crash structures front and rear. Twin liquid-cooled battery packs will sit low down and either side of the mid-mounted engine. They will be able to be charged either from a domestic supply, by regenerative braking, or from the engine, and they will give the C-X75 an electric-only range of 60km or 37.5 miles.

The aim is to bring the car to market in 2014. Just 200 will be made, and the price is expected to be £800,000.

# *Octane*
# INTERACTIVE

## THE WORLD'S GREATEST CLASSIC AND PERFORMANCE CARS AT YOUR FINGERTIPS

Octane Interactive iPad edition brings you unrivalled road and track tests along with stunning photography, expert writers and legendary columnists from around the world. Enjoy exclusive videos, sound effects and 360-degree scrollable interiors of the most revered classics on Octane Interactive today

# Koenigsegg CC85/CCX/CXR

## CARBON BODIES, TWIN-SUPERCHARGED V8s, UP TO 1000BHP – MEET THE KOENIGSEGG FAMILY

For several years after the McLaren F1 appeared, it seemed we'd never see its like again. The F1 was fast all right. But it wasn't supersonic. Why should it be allowed to rest in peace as the 'greatest supercar ever built?' Why give up at 231mph and 0-60mph in 3.2sec?

Why indeed. The F1 started something: the race to beat it. And one of the first out of the blocks was a 28-year-old

Swede called Christian von Koenigsegg. A self-taught engineer, CvK had, some years earlier, envisioned the perfect high performance sports car and, rather than sit around scanning the car mags for its arrival, decided to make it. Thus was the Koenigsegg CC8S born. It boasted slightly more power than the F1 (655bhp), slightly less weight (1100kg) and a fine drag coefficient in the region of 0.28-0.30. Estimated top speed was 242mph and the predicted 0-62mph time 3.2sec.

Project Koenigsegg was rolling. But it wasn't until 2005, when the car had evolved, via the CCR, into the CCX, that Koenigsegg's ambition was realised. Powered by Koenigsegg's own 806bhp 4.7-litre, twin-supercharged V8, the 1180kg carbonfibre supercar clocked 241mph on the bowl at Nardo in southern Italy, beating the previous record set by Jonathan Palmer in the McLaren F1 (231mph) and just pipping the F1's 240.1mph set with the rev-limiter removed at the VW test track.

With a shape that echoed the McLaren's sense of function, an interior from a slightly dysfunctional future and arguably the coolest doors of any car on the planet (they swivelled upwards *and* outwards, a bit like a ladybird's wing casings pre-flight) the CCX more than looked the part. On the move, it could lift the hairs on your neck with its mighty roar and savage delivery allied to a well-sorted and tactile chassis. As for the 2007 biofuel CCXR (1004bhp), exciting hardly covered it.

Koenigsegg was building its own engines by the time the CCX appeared. This one made 806bhp

# Koenigsegg Agera R

## THE AGERA IS THE LATEST 'EGG, AND THE R VERSION IS THE FASTEST AND MOST POWERFUL

For those days when 800, 900, even 1000 horsepower simply doesn't hit the spot, may we recommend the 5.0-litre Agera R, the car **evo** tester Chris Harris described as being 'about as fast and exciting as your body can handle'.

Not entirely unexpected when you consider that this 'hot' version of Koenigsegg's replacement for the CC has, when fuelled at the E85 bioethanol pump, 1100bhp, a power-to-weight ratio of 779bhp per ton and a claimed top speed of over 260mph. Harris found it beautifully built and surprisingly driveable for such a beast. While still clearly related to the CC-series, the Agera has a subtly revised body with improved aero, a whole host of changes inside, and a new, twin-turbo version of the previously supercharged Koenigsegg V8.

Agera is Swedish for 'act' so, appropriately, Koenigsegg took its

### SPECIFICATION

**Years made** 2011-
**Engine** V8, 5000cc, twin-turbo
**Max power** 1100bhp @6900rpm
**Torque** 885lb ft @4100rpm
**0-60mph** 2.9sec
**Max speed** 260+mph
**Price** c£875,000 new

**evo** RATING
★★★★★

fastest ever car and established a slew of new records. It covered the dash from 0-300kph (186mph) in 14.53sec, faster even than the 14.6sec recorded for the Veyron Super Sport. Zero to 200mph took just three seconds more, at 17.68 seconds, again besting the Bugatti. The performance tests also called on the Agera's gigantic 397mm (front) and 380mm (rear) carbon-ceramic brakes. This time stopping from 186mph and 200mph, the R posted 6.66 and 7.28sec respectively. Perhaps the most impressive figure of all was the 24.96sec it took the Agera R to cover 0-200-0mph.

In 2012, Koenigsegg began to export to new markets, including the States and China, where one customer took delivery of a special edition Agera R called the BLT (yes, really). With a blue-tinted clear carbon body and other unique features selected by its owner, it was evidence of a growing trend towards bespoke supercars, a trend also being embraced by Ferrari and McLaren.

Above: Koenigsegg paid plenty of attention to Agera's aero, and with good reason. Left: some seriously big numbers

# Lamborghini Miura

## A RACE-CAR ENGINE AND CHASSIS UNDER A SKIN OF UNIQUE BEAUTY, THAT WAS THE MIURA

The Miura is the Lamborghini you know you must drive before you die. Its reputation for being fast but flawed – not to mention fragile – might lead you to believe that indulgence in one act could bring about the premature arrival of the other. But that's all part of the dangerous fascination.

To be blunt, the Miura was a little 'over-engined'. Its quad-cam V12 was a development of the extraordinary 3.5-litre powerplant designed as a quasi-race unit by ex-Ferrari engineering wizard Giotto Bizzarrini. As well as twelve cylinders, four camshafts and six double-barrel carburettors, it possessed what looked like several miles of visceral chains. Naturally, all this sounded impressive enough from the outside. Inside it was plain loud.

By the time it appeared in the Miura – sensationally slung sideways across the middle – it had grown to 4 litres

and 350bhp. Gianpaulo Dallara's trend-setting configuration could be seen clearly in the 1965 Turin Show chassis mock-up. The actual car appeared at Geneva a year later. This time it was fully clothed by Bertone, the work of its new design genius, Marcello Gandini. It was a sensation, a radical departure from the front-engined superfast tourers that had come before it.

All of that said, the Miura was highly-strung and had a fragile disposition. In

its original form, the chassis would flex perceptibly during hard cornering. It also had a tendency to lift its nose at high speed, so that at anything above 150mph it could wander alarmingly – a tendency that was only partially cured with the later S and SV versions. Italians are chaotic, so are their cars. They also know what the magic of driving is and how to make it. In the end, that's all that matters. Some 45 years later, the Miura remains arguably the sexiest car ever made.

Above: driving position was what we politely call Italianate. Left: transversely mounted 4-litre V12 made 350bhp and up

# Lamborghini Countach

## NO SHAPE SAYS SUPERCAR MORE CLEARLY, BUT THE COUNTACH WAS ALSO A GREAT DRIVE

**M**ention the word 'supercar' to anyone with even a vague interest in the subject and even if the word doesn't immediately slip into the conversation, the image that will flicker into focus like a Derren Brown mind-plant will almost certainly be that of the Lamborghini Countach. As it was at its launch in 1974, it remains the shape that defines the genre, though by the time

the horribly over-embellished valedictory Anniversary edition appeared in 1990, Lamborghini had perhaps forgotten how outrageously perfect the unadorned original design was.

Indeed, it was conceived as a styling exercise, then adapted for use on the public highway – but its genesis was hijacked (thankfully) by people with an obsession for high performance and, for better or worse, motorsport. Its tubular steel chassis was delicate but

light and strong, as was the alloy body. The questionable space-efficiency of the Miura's transverse motor was ditched in favour of a longitudinal orientation for the V12 and from each corner hung a pair of wishbones. By the time it had morphed into the best version of all, the Quattrovalvole, it had grown taller but become more habitable too, allowing grown adults to sit upright in the cabin.

The quattrovalvole engine regularly saw 470bhp on the dyno and Ferrari's rival Testarossa felt slow by comparison. The QV's racing car origins shone through in the way it drove, with fully uni-balled suspension and a kerb weight of just 1447 kilos. Once up and running, the Countach was a blast, a cardiovascular gym session drenched in carburettor gurgle and rasping V12 overrun. Today, it's a reminder of what vast mechanical power used to feel like before powered controls and electronic assistance. A warm glow if you got it right, your own page on WreckedExotics if you didn't.

QV was probably the best Countach. The 48v engine was mighty, the chassis well-sorted

# Lamborghini Diablo

## THE DIABLO WAS BORN AT A TIME OF TURMOIL FOR LAMBO, BUT IT CAME RIGHT IN THE END

**L**ike the Miura and Countach before it, the Diablo was an end in itself, the antithesis of humdrum and mundane, pure and uncompromised in its ability to thrill. It wasn't an exercise in subtlety. But its development wasn't always straightforward.

Work had begun in 1986 and continued for the next four years. Early prototypes ran a mechanical four-wheel-drive set-up but it was crude and unreliable and the first production cars would revert to rear-wheel drive.

Lamborghini's new flagship simply had to be right. It had to move the game on from the Countach, and its chief weapons would be a more powerful engine and stronger brakes. With 492bhp, it was the world's fastest production car in 1990, hitting a verified top speed of 202mph. In one sense, job done. The Diablo had the style (courtesy of Marcello Gandini, naturally) and it had the speed.

But it was also pretty hard work, especially its unassisted steering. The VT version of 1993 brought four-wheel drive but, perhaps even more significantly, power steering.

The thing was, the Diablo's further development coincided with a turbulent time for Lamborghini the company. In 1987 it had been bought by Chrysler, then in 1994 by unsympathetic new Indonesian owners. Salvation came in the shape of Audi, who bought the company in 1998.

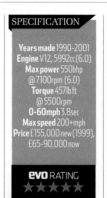

**SPECIFICATION**

**Years made** 1990-2001
**Engine** V12, 5992cc (6.0)
**Max power** 550bhp
@ 7100rpm (6.0)
**Torque** 457lb ft
@ 5500rpm
**0-60mph** 3.8sec
**Max speed** 200+mph
**Price** £155,000 new (1999),
£65-90,000 now

**evo** RATING
★★★★★

The final iteration of the Diablo, the 6.0 – the first to showcase Audi's engineering input – was dynamically polished, better even than the 'pure' Italian cars. Its engine was treated to variable valve timing and completely new calibration that made it a puppy dog at low revs but allowed it to remain a salivating psychopath at the top end. It was completely captivating. Not only had Lamborghini blossomed under Audi but somehow managed to become even more unhinged.

Above and left: the 'Audified' Diablo 6.0 was better built, but it was also every bit as mad as the old-school Lambos

# Lamborghini Murciélago

*LAMBO'S NEW FLAGSHIP FOR A NEW MILLENNIUM WAS JUST AS WILD AS ITS FOREBEARS*

**D**riving a Murciélago through the middle of a town was almost an act of civic beneficence. It was a kinetic sculpture that put the day's drudgery on hold, if only for a few seconds. Effortlessly cool, it didn't have to compete for attention. It didn't have to compete at all.

Take the LP640-4: 0-60mph in 3.3sec, 211mph flat-out. The performance was exciting, entertaining, accessible, the sensations it generated all-consuming and hugely addictive. From the beginning, the Murciélago's V12 was arguably the greatest ever to power a production car. Given its head on any decent straight, its push was unabatingly savage, gear after bellowing gear. And remember we're talking about an engine whose lineage stretches back some 40 years. And the Murciélago was the perfect showcase. Naturally, it was thunderously fast down the straights but also

## SPECIFICATION

**Years made** 2001-2011
**Engine** V12, 6496cc (LP670-4 SV)
**Max power** 661bhp @8000rpm
**Torque** 487lb ft @6500rpm
**0-60mph** 3.2sec
**Max speed** 212mph
**Price** £270,038 new (SV, 2011), £75-250,000 today

**evo** RATING
★★★★★

awesomely stable under braking, and precise and poised through the turns. The ride was firm but well controlled and the body structure felt vault-solid.

Then there was the LP670-4 SV – the definitive Murciélago and possibly the definitive supercar driving experience; the wildest ride, the seat to be in if you wanted your sensible world coordinates shredded and blown away. A savagely fast car, the SV hammered so much immediacy and raw excitement into the usual supercar mix – even as defined by the LP640 – your heart nearly leapt out of your chest. The modest 30bhp hike (making 661bhp) looked a lot more impressive in conjunction with the 100kg drop in weight. Factor-in a bodyshell, aerodynamics and suspension all reworked to generate more grip and suddenly Lamborghini's argument that, while a rear-drive Murcie looked good on paper, the SV actually *needed* its four-wheel drive to make good on its extra potential, didn't sound like a boast.

My, how you've grown. Lambo's V12 is now up to 6.5 litres and, in SV form, produces 661bhp

F1 DSL

*Lamborghini*

# Lamborghini Reventón

## THE MURCIÉLAGO-BASED REVENTÓN WAS A 1M-EURO LIMITED-EDITION WORK OF ART

How do you turn a Murciélago LP640 into something more extreme? Perhaps more to the point, why would you want to? Chances are, you wouldn't. But Lamborghini reckoned there had to be a least 20 people with a no-limit credit card who would. So it made the million-euro Reventón just for them – the most expensive and extreme roadgoing Lambo of them all. Not so much a Veyron-chaser, but rather 'a symbol of extreme exclusivity'.

The design took much of its inspiration from America's F-22 Raptor fighter-jet with its simple, angular shape, sharp edges and distinctive nose-forward canopy. Exported to the four-wheeled realm, this translated into a more technical and edgy looking Murciélago with interrupted lines and contorted panels to create a more dynamic play of light across its surfaces. The aerospace overtones accounted for the only offered

Above: Reventón's look was inspired by the Raptor fighter plane. TFT displays (right) also had an aeronautical feel

paint finish as well. Grey Barra was described as a 'mid-opaque grey without the usual shine'. Matt, in other words.

Inside, the dash had no dials, only three TFT liquid crystal displays. There was even a G-Force meter that represented dynamic driving forces, depending on the direction and intensity of the acceleration.

The Reventón drove pretty much exactly like a standard LP640, which was entirely to be expected because, under the skin, that's exactly what it was.

# Lamborghini Aventador LP700-4

## LAMBORGHINI'S CURRENT BIGGEST HITTER HAS AN ALL-NEW V12 AND MUCH MORE BESIDES

Designing a new car completely from scratch is extremely rare – principally because it's so darned expensive – but that's exactly what Lamborghini has done here. The problem was that the outgoing Murciélago's chassis, engine and running gear were all well past their use-by date, the mechanicals dating back to the prehistoric days when CO2 was something only discussed in school

classrooms and crash safety was down to the driver not crashing. Basically they had to bin everything and start again. The only sacrosanct areas were a mid-mounted V12 layout, four-wheel drive, and scissor doors – all deemed to be at the core of Lamborghini DNA.

The end result was the Aventador, launched in 2011, and claimed by Lamborghini to represent a jump of two generations in development terms. Unmistakeably a Lambo, it has all the

visual drama of its forebears, inside and out. But so much is new, from the 690bhp 6.5-litre V12 – the first completely new Lambo V12 since the first one, way back in the early '60s – to the ISR (independent shifting rod) single-clutch automated manual gearbox to the pushrod-based suspension.

The new V12 delivers its power in an utterly linear way as the revs build to a crescendo and the 8500rpm limit approaches. It's a monumentally quick car, but the delivery is never intimidating, while the sonic onslaught is utterly addictive – no change there then. The ceramic brakes are super-strong, the handling balanced and confidence-inspiring, encouraging you to drive at the limit – on track at least. Perhaps the only weakpoint is the gearbox, which isn't as quick and slick as the dual-clutchers used by Ferrari and others, though it does save a chunk of weight. Otherwise the Aventador is a triumph, as evidenced by the 18-month waiting list.

The first all-new Lambo V12 since... well, since the first one back in the early 1960s. It's suitably epic in delivery too

# Lamborghini Aventador J

## THIS ONE-OFF £1.75MILLION ROADSTER IS PERHAPS THE MOST OUTRAGEOUS LAMBO OF ALL

**I**f you thought the Reventón was just a little common, and maybe a little understated, then the Aventdaor J could be just the thing for you. Even for a manufacturer known for its outrageous cars, this is something special.

The 'J' refers to Appendix J, the section of the FIA rulebook that deals with motorsport homologation – just as it did 40 years ago for a very special one-off Miura created by celebrated Lamborghini test driver Bob Wallace.

And, just like the legendary Miura Jota, the extraordinary Aventador J is no fragile concept car. It is fully functional – underneath are the mechanics of a 'standard' Aventador, so that means the 690bhp 6.5-litre V12 and seven-speed paddleshift gearbox, though shedding the roof and consequently around 80kg gives an even more formidable power-to-weight ratio of about 470bhp per ton.

Top speed is quoted as in excess of

The way supercars always used to be – shocking, impractical, stupidly expensive, and utterly awesome

### SPECIFICATION

| | |
|---|---|
| **Years made** | 2012 |
| **Engine** | V12, 6498cc |
| **Max power** | 690bhp @8250rpm |
| **Torque** | 509lb ft @5500rpm |
| **0-60mph** | 2.8sec |
| **Max speed** | 186mph+ |
| **Price** | £1.75million |

**evo** RATING
★★★★★

300kph (186mph), though what it would feel like in the rush of air at that sort of speed, with no windscreen as such, almost defies imagination.

Sadly, it's very unlikely that we'll ever find out what it's like to drive, because the Aventador J is such a collector's piece that it's almost certainly destined to be secreted away in some dehumidified bunker. Apparently the buyer heard about the car and coughed up £1.75million without even seeing it...

# Lamborghini Gallardo

## IN 2003, LAMBORGHINI REVEALED A V10-ENGINED BABY BROTHER FOR THE MURCIÉLAGO

Back in 2003, no other manufacturer in the world boasted an all-wheel-drive, V10-engined, 192mph entry-level model, but then no other manufacturer in the world had Lamborghini's unrivalled reputation for building jaw-dropping supercars. Consequently, absurd as it may have seemed, the Gallardo was Lamborghini's baby. All 1440kg, 493bhp and £120,000-worth of it. Unmistakably Lambo, yet uncharacteristically trim and compact of form, the Gallardo managed to pack a quart's-worth of presence into a pint-sized supercar pot.

The seating position was low, backside just inches off the ground, windscreen arcing off into the distance, stubby nose diving out of sight, view ahead dominated by a neat, bubble-shaped instrument binnacle. It was an extreme driving environment: thick A-pillars partially obscuring your diagonal sight-lines, letterbox rear window and worrying over-the-shoulder blindspot. It was an authentic shrink-to-fit supercar interior, but with a hint of everyday useability.

Displacing 5 litres and delivering 493bhp and 376lb ft of torque, the Gallardo's dry-sumped, all-alloy V10 was one of the world's most potent production motors. In a first for Lamborghini, there was the choice of a conventional stick-shift six-speed or a sequential paddle-shift. Like the Murciélago, the Gallardo employed Lamborghini's Viscous Traction all-wheel

drive. It stayed with the Gallardo through all of its evolutionary phases, save for 2009's rear-drive LP550-2 Balboni. Power grew over the years, culminating in the 562bhp LP570-4. But in any Gallardo, a decent straight and a couple of fast sweepers was all that was needed to get you hooked. Thumb the 'Corsa' button on the centre console to open the throats of the exhaust, crack the windows down a few inches and indulge: supercar heaven was but a few throttle-blips away.

SPECIFICATION

Years made 2003-
Engine V10, 4961cc
Max power 562bhp @8000rpm (570-4)
Torque 398lb ft @6500rpm
0-60mph 3.5sec
Max speed 202mph
Price £178,560 (2010), c£120,000 used

**evo** RATING
★★★★★

Gallardo is most potent in LP570-4 Superleggera guise, its V10 engine (left) churning out an exhilarating 562bhp

# Lexus LFA

## THE JAPANESE LUXURY CAR MAKER HIT THE BULLSEYE WITH ITS VERY FIRST SUPERCAR

Nine years in development, the Lexus LFA dived straight in at the deep end. A no-holds-barred supercar with a £350,000 price tag, it isn't swimming with dolphins but the sharpest-toothed predators from Ferrari, Porsche and Lamborghini, all of which cost at least £100K less.

The first shock is its performance. With a 0-60mph time of 3.6sec and a 202mph top speed it is certainly quick – but both figures are bettered by less extravagantly priced rivals. The LFA is about far more than the figures, though. The quality of the car's construction and componentry is where the money seems to go. The bespoke, stratospherically high-revving normally aspirated 4.8-litre V10 in the nose is mated to a six-speed automated manual gearbox at the back, giving the LFA a near perfect 48/52 front/rear weight distribution.

Hi-tech lightweight construction is a

**SPECIFICATION**

Years made 2009-
Engine V10, 4805cc
Max power 552bhp
@8700rpm
Torque 354lb ft
@6800rpm
0-60mph 3.6sec
Max speed 202mph
Price £352,000 (new),
c£300,000 used

**evo** RATING
★★★★★

given, its CFRP (carbonfibre-reinforced polymer) chassis and bodywork offering four times the strength of aluminium at a saving of 100 kilos and giving the 1480kg car a potent 379bhp/ton power-to-weight ratio – better than a Ferrari 599's. Developed at the Nordschleife, its suspension is made mostly of aluminium to save further weight and the carbon-ceramic brakes shave even more from the unsprung mass.

But perhaps none of this really matters. From the futuristic kinetics of its sci-fi dashboard to its glass-shattering exhaust note at 9500rpm, the LFA looks, feels and sounds very special. And if the standard car wasn't quite special enough, in 2011 Lexus add the Nürburgring Edition, with an extra 10bhp, subtle aerodynamic tweaks and a run of just 50.

Not the fastest supercar, maybe, but fast enough. And utterly absorbing. Indeed when **evo** tested it against the Ferrari 599 GTO, we found the LFA the more intoxicating of the two.

Above: V10 sits way back in the chassis; with the rear-mounted gearbox it helps give the LFA near-perfect weight distribution

# Lister Storm

## THIS WAS THE ROAD VERSION OF LISTER'S TWIN-SUPERCHARGED V12 LE MANS CONTENDER

The original Lister car company had built Jaguar-based racers in the '50s and '60s. In the 1980s the name was revived by a new company that quickly made a name for building massively powerful and rather brutally restyled Jaguar XJ-Ss – but boss Laurence Pearce was already hatching much more ambitious plans...

Working out of an industrial unit in Leatherhead, Surrey, Lister Cars established itself, over the years, as the go-to outfit if you wanted your XJ-S to look a bit harder and go (quite a bit) faster. It wasn't the only company doing this, but the one thing you could rely on with Lister was the going faster thing. It knew its Jag V12 onions. Knew how much extra capacity and power the engines could take and remain reliable.

All of which must have been a little frustrating for Pearce because, while the XJ-S business kept the company

accountant happy, what he really wanted to do was build a racing car. So that's exactly what he did. The twin-supercharged 7-litre V12, front-engined, 2+2 Storm was conceived as an entrant in the GT1 class at the Le Mans 24-hours, with the homologation cars rolling straight into contention with the supercar elite on the road. With 0-60 in 4.1sec and a top speed of 208mph, it was for a while the world's fastest four-seater road car.

Unfortunately for Lister, the Storm proved an unreliable racer (on its debut at Le Mans in 1995 it managed just 40 laps) and, although it made a rapid, fine-handling road car, it cost £450,000 and it wasn't a Ferrari. Just four road versions were made, and only three are believed to survive today.

Lister continued to campaign versions of the Storm in a number of race series, winning the team championship in FIA GTs in 2000 and also enjoying some success in the British GT series before the cars were finally retired in 2006.

### SPECIFICATION

**Years made** 1993-1994
**Engine** V12, 6997cc, twin superchargers
**Max power** 594bhp @6000rpm
**Torque** 580lb ft @3500rpm
**0-60mph** 4.1sec
**Max speed** 208mph
**Price** V12, £450,000 (new), n/a (today)

**evo RATING**
★★★☆☆

The Storm wasn't a thing of great beauty, but its Jaguar underpinnings made it a practical and accomplished – if scarily expensive – super-GT

# Lotus Esprit

## TURBOCHARGING TURNED LOTUS'S STRIKING MID-ENGINED WEDGE INTO A TRUE SUPERCAR

The Esprit had been round since 1976, but it was the introduction of the Turbo model as an addition to the normally aspirated S2 (Series 2) Esprit in 1980 that signalled its arrival as a serious supercar, the 0-60 time tumbling to 5.6sec, the top speed climbing above 150mph, the always striking Giugiaro bodywork gaining skirts and spoilers and a whole new attitude.

With the Peter Stevens-redesigned S4 version introduced in 1987, the plastic-fantastic from Norfolk became the most spectacular celebration of intellect over muscle in supercardom. With just 2174cc and four cylinders, the turbocharged S4 developed a nominal 264bhp, although if running conditions were cool, the engine management allowed up to 280bhp – a staggering 120bhp more than the original, naturally aspirated S1. With a power-to-weight ratio of 232bhp/ton, the S4 could accelerate from zero to 60mph in around

**SPECIFICATION**

**Years made** 1980-2004
**Engine** V8, 3500cc, twin-turbo (Sport 350)
**Max power** 350bhp @ 6500rpm
**Torque** 295lb ft @ 4250rpm
**0-60mph** 4.3sec
**Max speed** 175mph
**Price** £66,135 new (1999), £30-£40,000 today (S350)

**evo** RATING
★★★★☆

4.7sec – faster than a Ferrari 512TR.

The S4 also had arguably the finest chassis of any Esprit, with cornering abilities a world apart from the S2 Turbo's. Turn-in was electric, grip borderline miraculous.

In its latter years, the Esprit was powered by a lightweight twin-turbo V8 and finally acquired the engine to do its brilliant chassis justice. Dramatic straight-line speed, phenomenal cornering power, stunning stoppers and responses that grew crisper, keener and more reassuring the harder you tried were the high points, a flat engine note and clunky gearchange the only real downsides.

Even at the very end with the be-winged Sport 350, when you only had to sit in one to know it was an old-school supercar with scattered, cheap switchgear, offset pedals, a cramped driving environment and poor visibility, the Esprit was all about driving dynamics, with handling and steering feel that were so pure they were still a match for any rival.

Perhaps the ultimate Esprit Turbo, the late-'90s Sport 350 featured a 3.5-litre twin-turbo V8 (right). Steering feel was among the very best

# Marussia B1/B2

## BASED ON EARLY IMPRESSIONS, RUSSIA'S FIRST SUPERCAR MANUFACTURER IS ONE TO WATCH

Marussia has become familiar to followers of Formula 1 in recent years, having taken over what was the Virgin Racing team, but it is also has ambitious plans to be a serious contender in the supercar market. The Russian company's first super-sports car, the B1, was unveiled in 2008, with sales starting in 2010. A second model, the B2, with the same mechanical package but wilder styling, followed, and the company has also launched a giant SUV called the F2.

The supercar – which Marussia sees as an alternative to the Ferrari 458 and Lamborghini Gallardo – is offered with three engine options, all designed by Cosworth (also suppliers for the Marussia F1 car). The base unit is a 3.5-litre naturally aspirated V6 producing 300bhp, but there is also a 2.8-litre turbo V6 offered in two states of tune: 360bhp and 420bhp. The engine is mounted

**SPECIFICATION**

**Years made** 2010-
**Engine** V6, 2800cc,
turbocharged
**Max power** 420bhp
@n/a rpm
**Torque** 442lb ft
@4000rpm
**0-60mph** 3.7sec
**Top speed** 155mph
**Price** c£110,000 (est)

**evo** RATING
★★★★☆

transversely amidships, driving the rear wheels through a six-speed paddleshift automatic gearbox.

Not huge power outputs, but with a central aluminium tub and steel spaceframes clad in carbonfibre body panels, the B1 weighs just 1100kg, which means that in its fiercest spec it has 388bhp/ton, which just pips the 458 Italia. Since **evo** has yet to test the car, we'll have to take the performance figures on trust, but 0-60mph in 3.7sec sounds entirely feasible.

Marussia claims to have sold its initial planned production run of 500 cars, which are being built at the Valmet factory in Finland. It's a huge ask to compete with the might of Ferrari and Audi-owned Lamborghini, but Marussia, led by Russian TV personality Nikolay Fomenko, isn't short of ambition. In May 2012 it opened a showroom in Monaco, its first outside Russia, and it plans further expansion in Europe, followed by the Middle East and Asia.

Left: B2 model has wilder styling but same engines. Above: prototype had a sophisticated infotainment system with plasma screens

# Maserati Bora

## YEARS BEFORE VW ADOPTED THE NAME, MASERATI'S BORA WAS THIS 177MPH BEAUTY

Maserati had enjoyed a golden age in the 1950s and '60s, both on the track and with high-performance GTs like the original Ghibli. But it wasn't until the early '70s that it produced arguably its first proper supercar.

The Bora, named after an energetic breeze local to the eastern Adriatic coast, was notable for being the first Maserati road car with its engine in the middle.

Some engine it was, too: the gloriously bellowing 90-degree V8 from the Ghibli, initially with a capacity of 4.7 litres, then, from 1974, 4.9 litres.

Also pinched from the Ghibli was its designer, Giorgetto Giugiaro, who won out against Pietro Frua in the competition to clothe the Maserati flagship. An impressively solid piece of work it was, too, and not just because Giugiaro was pretty much at the top of his game. The Bora always managed to look heavy

### SPECIFICATION

**Years made** 1971-1978
**Engine** V8, 4930cc
**Max power** 330bhp @5500rpm
**Torque** 325lb ft @4000rpm
**0-60mph** 6.6sec
**Max speed** 177mph
**Price** £9862 new, c£70-£100,000 today

**evo** RATING
★★★☆☆

from any angle (it was), an impression heightened when the similar but much daintier V6-engined Merak followed a year after the Bora's 1971 launch.

Back in the 1970s, Maserati was owned by Citroën, so the Bora made use of the French manufacturer's hydraulic system to operate the brakes, pop-up headlamps, driver's seat adjustment and the adjustable pedal-box. It made for a rather odd old-school-brute-force-meets-idiosyncratic-French-tech driving experience, but that didn't stop it becoming a must-have set of wheels for the rich and famous. Customers included Karim Aga Khan and Sophia Loren's hubby, movie producer Carlo Ponti.

Sadly, after this 1970s flowering of special Maseratis, in the '80s it all went a bit wobbly with a succession of plain-looking, small-capacity turbos. But in recent years, with a little help from Ferrari, it has enjoyed another resurgence. And that tie-up has also given us the most spectacular Maser of all...

Right: Giugiaro-styled Bora was Maserati's 1970s entry into the supercar market, with the Ghibli's V8 engine placed amidships

# Maserati MC12

A kissing cousin to the Ferrari Enzo and costing over half a million pounds when it was new, the 621bhp Maserati MC12 certainly put some vim and supercar credibility back into the famous brand.

Built on the Enzo platform, the Maserati's external dimensions were significantly larger in every direction but achieved a lower drag coefficient and, thanks to its carbon construction, it weighed just 1335kg. Despite its Group C racer stylings, it wasn't an intimidating car to drive. And it was surprisingly refined, too.

Yes, you could hear its big V12 working hard, but the word you'd use to describe it was 'restrained' rather than 'raw'. But for the fact that its luggage capacity amounted to whatever you could stuff into your pockets, it would have made a fine long-distance travelling companion.

All right, there was no stereo and some

## SPECIFICATION

**Years made** 2004-2005
**Engine** V12, 5998cc
**Max power** 621bhp @7500rpm
**Torque** 481lb ft @5500rpm
**0-60mph** 3.8sec
**Max speed** 205mph
**Price** £501,365 new, c£600-£1,000,000+ today

### evo RATING
★★★★☆

of the race-car hardware was barely disguised: the exposed roll-over bar, the black-painted bulkhead behind the seats. But the fundamentals were spot on. It was easy to get properly positioned behind the wheel in a superbly supportive seat, the controls were well positioned and the relatively upright, slightly bowed A-pillars made it easy to see out and accurately position the car. It was a supercar in which you could knock over Maidstone to Maranello in a day and not feel unduly shattered. If you could take in a circuit or two, so much the better.

That, after all, was its raison d'etre – to compete in the FIA GT Championship. The MC12 marked Maserati's return to racing after 37 years and it did this with notable success. GT1 MC12s began competing towards the end of 2004 and were soon scoring podium finishes, winning the manufacturers' cup in 2005. For the road, a production run of 30 cars was undertaken in 2004, with a further 25 rolling off the line the following year.

Under the skin, the MC12 was largely Enzo, including the 6-litre V12 engine. Extended body was all part of the aero package to go racing

# McLaren F1

The F1 has a special place – perhaps a unique place – in the story of the supercar. The singularity of the vision of Gordon Murray meant that nothing before, and very little since, comes close to its purity, its lack of compromises, and most of all its obsessive rejection of unnecessary weight and frippery.

Nowhere was that uniqueness more tangible than in its central driving position. The symmetry, the exceptional visibility, the feeling that you were at the very heart of things, that the car was built around you, the driver.

The tractability of the 6.1-litre V12 was such that it was possible to go up through the box on tickover, and then floor the throttle in sixth without the merest hint of a stumble or a murmur of protest. This was an exquisitely tuned monster of an engine, and even pulling a top gear good for over 230mph (240mph with the rev limiter removed),

the F1 would soon pick up pace and strike out for the horizon, an irresistible combination of big-capacity torque and minimal weight.

The lack of flywheel effect in the engine ensured that the revs flared and died back almost instantly, which was another factor in the F1's amazingly crisp, clean throttle response. It also meant you had to be positive and accurate with the gearshift, clutch and throttle; conducting the McLaren smoothly demanded finesse,

but the satisfaction of getting it just-so was ample reward. Even at modest speeds, the steering was perfectly weighted and brimming with texture.

The ride was surprisingly supple too. Despite the F1 name and the motorsport experience behind its design and construction, it was no racer in disguise. And yet a polished, instantly responsive feel permeated the F1, and the level of feedback and feel it delivered remains unmatched by any other supercar.

### SPECIFICATION

**Years made** 1994-1998
**Engine** V12, 6064cc
**Max power** 627bhp @7500rpm
**Torque** 479lb ft @4000-7000rpm
**0-60mph** 3.2sec
**Max speed** 231mph
**Price** £634,500 new, £2million+ today

**evo** RATING
★★★★★

*F1's simple shape and lack of adornment have helped it to age well. It never shouted its credentials, but then it didn't need to*

# McLaren MP4-12C

## THE FIRST OF A NEW GENERATION OF McLAREN ROAD CARS, THE MP4-12C IS A TOUR DE FORCE

**M**cLaren's mission for the MP4-12C could hardly have been much clearer. It wasn't to slug it out with the Ferrari 458 Italia, Lamborghini Gallardo, Porsche 911 GT2 RS and Audi R8 V10 in a still-recovering supercar market. It was to teach them a lesson (especially the Ferrari). How? With an unprecedented transfer of F1 construction, technology and computer simulation-aided development from track to road. It was what the Woking-based operation knew best; we expected nothing less.

Predictably, the 'C' in the name stood for carbon, specifically the car's spectacularly light and strong carbonfibre 'MonoCell' tub, which brought the technology of F1 to a sub-£200K road car where it had usually been the preserve of just a few hypercars like the Veyron, Zonda and Koenigsegg.

The MP4-12C is powered by an all-new, purpose-built 3.8-litre, dry-sumped, twin-turbo V8 with variable valve timing and a flat-plane crank. It develops 592bhp and revs to a Ferrari-matching 8500. But that's just the start. Then there's the seven-speed dual-clutch gearbox with Pre-Cog, and brake-steer, and the suspension which is hydraulically supported and connected and has adaptive dampers but no anti-roll bars. So it's quite unlike anything we've seen before. But is it better?

The twin-turbo V8 delivers a ferocious

punch; so much so that very few rivals can live with the 12C, especially when the surface gets challenging, because the sophisticated suspension soaks up lumps and undulations like no other.

Great visibility, compact dimensions, subtle styling that won't attract the wrong sort of attention, excellent refinement – it's a very useable supercar, capable of devouring great distances. Maybe the 458 Italia has more passion, but the 12C is a towering achievement.

### SPECIFICATION

| | |
|---|---|
| **Years made** | 2011- |
| **Engine** | V8, 3799cc, twin-turbo |
| **Max power** | 592bhp @7000rpm |
| **Torque** | 442lb ft @3000-7000rpm |
| **0-60mph** | 3.0sec |
| **Max speed** | 205mph |
| **Price** | £176,000 new, £150-200,000 used |

**evo RATING**
★★★★★

12C shares the F1's lack of showiness and also its depth of engineering. For McLaren's 'entry-level' model it's also mind-alteringly rapid

# McLaren P1

## THIS IS THE TRUE SUCCESSOR TO THE F1. FROM WHAT WE KNOW, IT'S GOING TO BE AWESOME

One of the few figures that McLaren has so far divulged for its new flagship supercar is already enough to leave our appetites thoroughly whetted. It will have over 600bhp per tonne – and the significant thing about that is that it tops even the legendary F1.

While officially a design study, the P1 is clearly the company's new hypercar, previously only known by its development codename P12, and set to do battle with the new-age Ferrari Enzo next year.

What else do we know? That the large rear wing adjusts automatically to provide maximum downforce when needed. That there is an F1-inspired drag reduction system for increased straight-line speed, with various movable flaps underneath the car, and a certain amount of 'Ground Effects' from the flat floor. It all adds up to a claimed 600kg of downforce at fast road speeds, which is about the same as the 12C GT3 racer has.

McLaren MD Antony Sheriff says the P1's goal is not to be the fastest, but to be 'the most exciting, most capable, most technologically advanced and most dynamically accomplished supercar ever made'. While not confirmed, the P1 is expected to use a heavily revised version of the MP4-12C's 3.8-litre twin-turbo V8, delivering around 750bhp. It'll be complemented by a Formula 1-style KERS electric motor, which will operate through the dual-clutch gearbox and boost the

**SPECIFICATION**

Years made 2013-
Engine V8, 3799cc, twin-turbo (tbc)
Max power c750bhp (tbc)
Torque c550lb ft (tbc)
0-60mph c2.5sec (tbc)
Max speed 200mph+ (tbc)
Price c£800,000

**evo RATING**
★★★★★

total power output to around 850bhp.

Much under the skin will be related to the MP4-12C, including the 'ProActive Chassis Control' suspension set-up and the carbon tub. So the P1 will be similar in dimensions to the 12C, though it's fair to say it possesses rather more presence. Further details will be announced early in 2013, shortly before sales begin with a price tag of around £800,000. Deliveries are due to commence in late 2013, the year of McLaren's 50th anniversary.

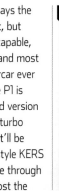

Opposite: huge rear aerofoil and venturis are the most obvious evidence of the P1's aero technology, which will set a new road car benchmark

# Mercedes-Benz SLR McLaren

## WHEN MERC AND McLAREN COMBINED FORCES, THE RESULTS WERE FLAWED BUT STILL FAB

How the SLR ended up as an object of mild ridicule associated with desperate, attention-seeking celebrities rather than a serious sequel to the phenomenal McLaren F1 is a long and painful story. It's also one that Gordon Murray – captain and opening bat for McLaren at the beginning of the project – would probably rather forget. Suffice to say, it wasn't the car he envisaged.

Murray's dream of a V12 was canned early on in favour of a supercharged 5.5-litre V8 mated to a five-speed auto. What's more, the production car had to remain true to the extraordinarily dramatic Vision SLR concept of 1999, lousy aerodynamics included. This necessitated quite a bit of 'correction', some of it out of view (the flat underbody) and some of it not (the rear diffuser and 'air brake'-style active rear wing). McLaren's chief contribution was the hugely rigid carbon

### SPECIFICATION

**Years made** 2004-2007
**Engine** V8, 5439cc, supercharged
**Max power** 617bhp @6500rpm
**Torque** 575lb ft @3250rpm
**0-60mph** 3.7sec
**Max speed** 208mph
**Price** £313,565 new, c£120-£250,000 today

**evo** RATING
★★★★☆

tub, adapted from its F1 expertise and, indeed, the F1 road car.

The SLR's signature scissor doors that swung out and up on massive hydraulic struts gave easy access to cabin space that checked in somewhere between cosy and cramped. Those who held off for the subsequent roadster arguably got the better car. With the powered fabric hood stowed neatly in the space behind the seats, it was a fabulous looking thing and still a fireball of presence with dragster overtones and stubby, side-firing exhausts snorting shockwaves of infrabass venom. Pure theatre.

Whichever the model, the SLR covered the distance between one corner and the next like a striking cobra covers the distance between itself and lunch.

For all its foibles, driving the SLR was an event that lingered in the emotions hours after you'd walked away. The car F1 partners Mercedes and McLaren built may not have been a great supercar but it was a phenomenon all the same.

SLR came in both coupe and convertible versions, and the roadster was arguably the better car, all the better to enjoy the bombastic V8

# Mercedes-Benz SL65 AMG Black

## *WITH EVEN MORE POWER THAN THE SLR, THIS WAS AMG SHOWING ITS WICKED SIDE*

The SL65 Black has the presence of a flame-thrower in a ticker-tape factory. It doesn't even look much like the car it's based on. Apart from the grille, lights and doors, the SL bits have been completely subsumed by the mostly carbon Black Series bits, which add girth, attitude, price and exclusivity in unprecedented quantities but, via some clever re-engineering and ditching the folding

Vario roof for a fixed one, cleave a handy 250 kilos from the kerb weight, too.

You'd imagine that the benefit of this – along with a hand-built 6.0-litre twin-turbo V12 generating 661bhp at 5400rpm and a capped torque output of 737lb ft between 2200 and 4200rpm (otherwise it would be a transmission-trashing 900lb ft plus) plus a completely re-worked chassis – would be hard to overestimate.

But despite its visual potency and turbo-massaged firepower, the SL65

**SPECIFICATION**

**Years made** 2009-2010
**Engine** V12, 5980cc, twin turbochargers
**Max power** 661bhp @5400rpm
**Torque** 737lb ft @2200-4200rpm
**0-60mph** 3.8sec
**Max speed** 199mph (limited)
**Price** £250,000 new, c£200,000 today

**evo** RATING
★★★★☆

Black lacks the true drama of a full-on mid-engined supercar. It has a curiously calm aura, an implied 'don't make me angry, you wouldn't like me when I'm angry' threat, but securely locked away until needed. The cabin is much like any other SL's. The aluminium paddles provoke a twinge of extra excitement, but then you remember they're hooked up to Merc's old five-speed auto – albeit with uprated hydraulics for faster shift speeds – rather than the properly sophisticated seven-speed semi-auto from the much cheaper SL63 AMG.

Then there's the sonic contribution of the engine, which seems to have no mechanical 'edge' at all, merely numerous, minutely varied layers of 'whoomph'. It's subdued from the inside, too, and fails to make the electrical connection with the small hairs on the back of your neck. For all its jaw-dropping pace and sensational on-road presence, the SL65 Black is neither a hardcore track tool nor a truly inspiring supercar.

AMG's thorough reworking of the SL extended from the monstrous twin-turbo V12 (left) to even ditching the folding top in favour of a fixed roof

# Mercedes-Benz SLS AMG

## THE RETURN OF THE GULLWING MERCEDES WAS A TRIUMPH FOR THE MEN FROM AMG

Two things strike you immediately about the SLS coupe. The first is those gullwing doors, the second is the noise. Even on a light throttle overrun, the SLS delights with a rumble and crackle like distant thunder and lightning as unburnt fuel ignites in the exhaust. Of course, this evocative soundscape is entirely engineered, but it shows that the chaps at AMG truly love the traditional offset-crank V8. And they've gone to great lengths to ensure that the 6.2-litre V8, designed specifically for Mercedes' AMG models, sounds at its very best in the SLS, the first car for which the Affalterbach outfit is entirely responsible.

With a front-mid-engined layout and largely aluminium construction, it's a hugely impressive machine, with a broad range of talents and bags of charisma. Perhaps its only slightly weakpoint is the tardy response of its gearbox – it's a beefed-up version of the Getrag twin-clutch transaxle used in the Ferrari California, but while it's smooth and swift in auto mode, use the paddles and there's a frustrating delay. That apart, the SLS is deeply impressive. There's an easy, natural feel to the well-weighted steering, and the ride (with fixed dampers, nothing fancy here) combines fine body control with the right degree of compliance. It steers accurately, and although it's a big car, once you're travelling at speed that doesn't seem to be an issue.

### SPECIFICATION

Years made 2010-
Engine V8, 6208cc
Max power 563bhp
@6800rpm
Torque 479lb ft
@4750rpm
0-60mph 3.7sec
Max speed 197mph (limited)
Price £168,395 new,
c£100-160,000 used

**evo** RATING
★★★★★

Over fast, flowing roads it feels simply brilliant, dealing tightly with crests and compressions, all four corners planted. AMG has nailed the dynamics beautifully, and the SLS delivers long-distance refinement too. Add in deep-chested, characterful performance and traffic-stopping looks, and not even a tardy twin-clutcher can spoil the party. You can even have it as a convertible. The roadster loses none of the coupe's prowess – but it does lose those doors...

From its gorgeous interior (left) to its thunderous, naturally aspirated V8, the SLS is a compelling and uniquely stylish supercar. We love it

AR08 MMC

# Morgan AeroMax

*MORGAN'S TAKE ON A SUPER-SPORTS CAR WAS TYPICALLY ECCENTRIC AND RATHER COOL*

For years, decades even, nothing very much changed at Morgan. Occasionally they'd introduce a new engine, though often only because the last one had gone out of production. But then, round about the turn of the millennium, things started to change. First there was the Aero, with its extruded aluminium chassis and BMW V8. But even that couldn't prepare us for what came next.

evo got its first taste of the AeroMax in 2005, just after its debut at the Geneva motor show. Designed by Matt Humphries, a 21-year-old design student, that first car was a one-off created for a Swiss banker who'd funded most of Morgan's GT3 racing. After the reception it received at the show there was never any doubt that more would be made.

BMW's 4.8-litre V8 put out a hefty 362bhp, endowing the 1180kg Morgan a very healthy power-to-weight ratio of 312bhp per ton and an impressive 0-62mph time of 4.2sec. To drive, the Max felt like it looked: quite unlike anything else (OK, except an Aero 8).

The sensation through the steering wheel was much like the impression given by the view over the bonnet, that the front wheels were a long way out ahead. You had to think slightly further down the road than you were used to, and pour the distant nose of the car into a corner sometime before you – sitting over the back wheels – actually arrived there.

SPECIFICATION

Years made 2008-10
Engine V8, 4799cc
Max power 362bhp
@6300rpm
Torque 370lb ft
@3600rpm
0-60mph 4.2sec
Max speed 170mph
Price £110,000 new,
c£110,000 today

evo RATING
★★★★⯪

There was something indefinably vintage about the experience, but as the miles slipped underneath you the Morgan revealed a very modern level of grip. So all that creamily delivered BMW urge was certainly exploitable. And very engaging.

Wealthy enthusiasts including Richard Hammond and Rowan Atkinson clearly agreed and bought AeroMaxes of their own. The production run, limited to 100 cars, ended in 2010, but the AeroMax effect will last a lot longer.

Building on the success of the Aero roadster, the AeroMax with its stunning fastback body featured a 362bhp BMW V8

# Mosler MT900S/PHOTON

## A RACE-BRED SUPERCAR WITH AN AMERICAN HEART AND A BRIT-DEVELOPED CHASSIS

**W**hat, you might ask yourself, is a Mosler? Good question. If you're a fan of British GT racing, you'll know the answer: a highly effective, lightweight, mid-engined, V8 supercar from the US (but also made in the UK) designed principally for a life on the track but, for those into a bit of harmless Porsche and Ferrari driver ego-destruction, produced in road-going form, too.

Florida-based Mosler Automotive was founded in 1985 by Warren Mosler and has produced a series of race-cars with roadgoing siblings. The MT900 and its S variant were the original roadgoing versions of Mosler's GT3-category racer. The job of developing the car for European fell to Norfolk-based Breckland Technologies, and the latest iteration is the Photon. None of them is exactly what you'd call sophisticated, though they do at least have air-conditioning.

**SPECIFICATION**

**Years made** 2004-
**Engine** V8, 5665cc
**Max power** 435bhp
@6300rpm (MT900S)
**Torque** 375 lb ft
@4000rpm
**0-60mph** 3.1sec
**Max speed** 200mph
**Price** £100,000 new,
c£50-£80,000 used

**evo** RATING
★★★★☆

So it's pretty much a pukka racer – think ultra-lightweight Corvette with its engine in the middle – minus the roll-cage, with more tread on the tyres and a 911 GT3-sourced six-speed 'box as an alternative to the Hewland sequential straight-cut-cog item.

The essence of the roadgoing Mosler is that of a barely diluted track car with a brutal kick (0-60 in around 3sec, the ton in a fraction over 7), well-balanced handling and absolutely tons of grip. Raw and loud and in-yer-face, proudly track-reared and a few steps removed from your regular supercar experience.

The Photon, introduced in 2011, saw power jump to 550bhp. When **evo** drove it, we found it delivered instant thrust wherever you were in the rev-range. We also found the handling superb, quickly inspiring confidence to push it hard, get it up on its toes, to explore its limits and a few of your own. With Warren Mosler's impending retirement from motorsport, it was a hell of a way to go out.

www.racinggreenmosler.co.uk

Left: MT900S was a roadgoing version of Mosler's GT3 racer. Photon derivative (right) saw power jump to 550bhp

# Nissan R390 GT1

## THE CURRENT GT-R DOESN'T QUITE CUT IT AS A SUPERCAR, BUT THIS NISSAN CERTAINLY DID

Comfortably as the GT-R sits on pole in any grid of Nissan's fastest cars from the past ten years, it isn't the fastest Nissan road car ever. The R390 GT1 is.

Back in the mid-1990s, Nissan's motorsport arm, Nismo, needed a new contender for sportscar racing – and that meant building a roadgoing version to satisfy the regulations. Good news for supercar fans...

Unlike most other GT1 projects with designs on Le Mans, Nissan built the road car necessary for homologation first and developed the racer from it. The work of Ian Callum, now design boss at Jaguar, and Tom Walkinshaw Racing, the R390 GT1 bore a certain resemblance to the Walkinshaw-built (but Peter Stevens styled) Jaguar XJR-15 but looked none the worse for that.

It was powered by Nissan's VRH35L twin-turbo 3.5-litre V8, fed by electronic

| SPECIFICATION | |
| --- | --- |
| Years made | 1997-1999 |
| Engine | V8, 3490cc, twin turbochargers |
| Max power | 550bhp @6800rpm |
| Torque | 470lb ft @4400rpm |
| 0-60mph | 3.9sec |
| Max speed | 200mph |
| Price | £642,000 new |

**evo RATING**
★★★★★

sequential port fuel injection, developing 550bhp at 6800rpm while still complying with all European market exhaust gas regulations. With the assistance of a launch control system and traction control, the R390 GT1 could hit 60mph from rest in under 4 seconds.

Underneath the all-carbonfibre structure was double wishbones all round, inboard dampers and front and rear anti-roll bars. Braking was handled by huge AP 14in vented front and rear disc brakes with six-piston calipers and ABS. Inside, the short-throw gear lever for the Xtrac six-speed sequential gearbox and tiny racing steering wheel were reminders of the close alliance between the road car and the racer.

Only two road R390s were built, along with eight racers. In competition, the R390 was up against the likes of the Porsche GT1, and the 1998 Le Mans would be its finest hour (all 24 of them), capturing four out of the top ten spots, including third just behind the GT1s.

Nissan's racing arm, Nismo, built the R390. The road version was purely an homologation exercise for racing

# Noble M600

## LIGHTWEIGHT CARBONFIBRE STRUCTURE, 650BHP TWIN-TURBO V8 AND A CHASSIS TO DIE FOR

Noble has been around since 1999, but founder Lee Noble departed in 2008. The first post-Noble Noble is the M600, and it's brilliant. Current boss, serial supercar owner Peter Dyson described the M600 as having the spirit and purity of a Ferrari F40, a decent-sized boot and enough power to hold its own in today's supercar landscape. Not only does that sound like the dreamiest of impossible dreams, it also happens to be true. If somewhat modest.

Consider: a stealthy, low-slung, mid-engined supercar powered by a twin-turbo V8 with roll-on acceleration not far short of a Veyron's, the F40's analogue purity, but a more benign, exploitable and forgiving demeanour. That's a wish list with an awful lot of ticks.

In terms of sheer speed, the M600 has few peers. When we staged a straight-line shootout between M600, McLaren MP4-12C, Ferrari 458, Merc SLS, 911

Turbo S and Ford GT, from 0-150mph the Noble was quicker than any of them (15.2sec for the record). And on a circuit against the 12C and 458, it was trading tenths with its technically far more sophisticated rivals.

That's hugely impressive, but looking beyond the stopwatch times, what really impressed **evo** about the M600 was the way it combined genuine race-car pace with a dynamic demeanour more forgiving and exploitable than just about

### SPECIFICATION

**Years made** 2009-
**Engine** V8, 4439cc, twin turbochargers
**Max power** 650bhp @ 6800rpm
**Torque** 604lb ft @ 3800rpm
**0-60mph** 3.0sec
**Max speed** 225mph
**Price** from £200,000 new

**evo** RATING
★★★★★

any of its rivals. But not in a Veyron/Nissan GT-R kind of way. You didn't have to be preternaturally talented to go fast in the M600, but the more you put into it, the more you got out. Rear-drive, no ABS or ESP, after all.

What makes it so special is the sublime steering and the utterly sussed nature of the chassis: its marriage of fantastic grip and traction (within reason), progressive transient manners and great ride. In short, it's absolutely phenomenal.

M600 does without a lot of electronic driver aids. What it does have is a naturally brilliant chassis and stunning performance

# Pagani Zonda

## JUST AS LAMBORGHINI CAME FROM NOWHERE IN THE 1960s, SO PAGANI 40 YEARS LATER

So the Pagani Zonda. From the C12S to the Cinque Roadster, it was always the same. Nought to naked desire in the time it took to walk up to it, open the stubby door, swing your torso into the lean, cupping embrace of the seat, slide it into a comfortable position and catch an eyeful of that extraordinary aluminium, leather and carbonfibre dash with its sci-fi instrument console and fabulous, retro-chic switches. Just twist the key that slipped the latch on the door to 555 horsepower (or 602 in the F, or 669 in the Cinque) and drive away. Make that rumble away, like thunder. And all the vision of a slight, bespectacled, quietly spoken Argentinean called Horacio Pagani.

Of all the Zondas, the F Roadster was probably *evo*'s favourite to drive (outside of the shock-and-awe fest that was the 739bhp Zonda R track car, of course). A power output of 602bhp may not sound overly excessive in 2011, but the F, like all Zondas, was light for a senior league exotic, at 1400kg. Snap open the throttle in just about any gear and that lack of inertia was even more apparent, the car lunging forward seemingly before the pedal had hit the stop.

High gears were fun, too, especially if you wanted to explore the V12's wonderful vocal repertoire in detail, from the heavy, churning, guttural pulse close to idle, through the sudden and shockingly open-throated bellow at 3000rpm, to the frantic yowl as the V12 keened to 7000rpm.

Even if you stripped away the exotic curves and the aura of awe that enveloped a Zonda, just the sight of the 7.3-litre V12, built by Mercedes' AMG go-faster department, sitting in the cradle of the steel spaceframe was enough to make grown men weep. Overwhelming, shattering, utterly addictive, the Zonda made you wonder if other supercar makers were just playing at it.

Zonda evolution reached a high with the F, especially in Roadster form. Such ferocious power, but so much tactility too

# Pagani Zonda 760RS

## 2012 SAW THE ZONDA REACH ITS ULTIMATE ROADGOING FORM WITH THE AWESOME 760

The Zonda story was supposed to end with the 669bhp Cinque, but wealthy customers kept pestering Horacio Pagani for a roadgoing version of the track-only Zonda R, so eventually he caved in and started developing the car you see here, the mighty Zonda 760RS – or 'Las Bestia' (The Beast) as it's affectionately known at Pagani.

The heart of it is a specially fettled version of the AMG 7.3-litre V12, producing a stupendous 750bhp (or 760PS, hence the name) and mated to a new seven-speed paddle-shift gearbox.

It's all clothed in fabulously glossy bare carbonfibre. The rear spoiler is even higher and wider than on the Cinque, and just as striking are the new dorsal fin, designed to smooth out the airflow, and the elongated air intake that snakes its way from the top of the windscreen back towards the mighty V12. Wider wheels

**SPECIFICATION**

Years made 2012
Engine V12, 7291cc
Max power 750bhp
@6300rpm
Torque 575lb ft
@4000rpm
0-60mph 2.9sec
Max speed 225mph
Price £1,500,000

**evo** RATING
★★★★★

(10in across at the front, 13in at the rear) necessitated wheelarch extensions, and there are small winglets on the sides of the snout to deflect air away from the turbulence caused by the wheels themselves. It looks simply stunning.

On the road it has huge, slightly menacing presence, and an epic soundtrack that rises to a piercing howl in the upper reaches of the rev-range (the red line has been raised by 500rpm to 7500). The increased power combined with reduced weight – thanks to Pagani's new construction technique for the carbon body panels and new titanium suspension components – brings a new layer of ferocity to the Zonda's acceleration, without losing the low-down torque and the exemplary ride that makes any Zonda such an easy companion.

Horacio Pagani has said he will make at least two more Zondas with the 760PS engine: one is believed to have been sold to Lewis Hamilton. If they really are the last of the line, what a swansong.

Wealthy customers of Pagani demanded a road version of the track-only Zonda R, and that's exactly what they got

# Pagani Huayra

## THE NEW HUAYRA IS A CLEAN-SHEET DESIGN WITH A TWIN-TURBO V12. AND IT'S SENSATIONAL

The exquisite Huayra – Pagani's 700bhp successor to the Zonda – is more than an incremental evolution of the car that, out of nowhere, took the supercar world by storm in 1999. Not only does it look very different, it's significantly more efficient and advanced.

It's powered by a 6.0-litre twin-turbo V12 made exclusively for the car by AMG, driving the rear wheels via a seven-speed single-clutch automated manual paddle-shift gearbox from Xtrac which weighs less than a double-clutch transmission and helps keep the overall kerb weight down to just 1390kg.

Seven years in the making, the Huayra has more than 4000 new components, excluding the engine and gearbox. The new car is longer than the Zonda, with a track increased by 70mm and the cabin position shifted 40mm back to liberate more room. The new car's profile is softer and simpler than the Zonda's but

Above: computer-controlled flaps (there are two more at the front) balance airflow and downforce on all four corners of the car

incorporates similar elliptical shapes for continuity of brand identity – likewise the central exhaust cluster.

In a supercar first, the Huayra's aero includes four computer-controlled flaps that, in conjunction with the active front suspension, are activated on the move to optimally balance airflow and downforce on all four corners of the car. The Huayra's tub is constructed from a carbon-titanium composite exclusive to Pagani. Suspension is a race-type pushrod setup, with adjustable Ohlins dampers and aluminium alloy wishbones.

Before anyone outside Zonda had experienced the Huayra (pronounced 'Why-ra'), reservations centred on whether a turbocharged engine could ever match the immediacy of response and the goosebump-inducing aural quality of the Zonda's naturally aspirated V12. And then there were the looks, and specifically what was unkindly described as the Huayra's 'guppy' face...

Well, in the raw, the Huayra is jaw-

dropping and just gets better the longer you stare at it. Those elegant teardrop wing mirrors, the head-swirling rims with spokes that get progressively more twisted, the lines that flow like honey from front to rear and finish in exquisitely bold shapes, the way the body seems stretched tight over its carbon-titanium chassis like an Adrian Newey F1 car... Even the most ardent Zonda fan will eventually be won over by the Huayra, which just seems so much more modern, and more exciting too. And that's before they've even driven it...

The single-clutch gearshift (Pagani couldn't bear the thought of a heavy twin-clutch arrangement sat at the rear of the car) feels a little ponderous at manoeuvring speeds, but once you're up and running it delivers rapid, decisive shifts. Meanwhile the ride has the familiar Zonda suppleness with underlying firmness and control, the ideal blend.

Best of all, throttle response is superb, immediately quelling any fears that the twin-turbocharged engine might not match the Zonda's naturally aspirated V12 for reaction time.

Above: ignition is achieved by inserting a Huayra-shaped 'key' into the dash. Gear selector is pure Pagani craftsmanship

## SPECIFICATION

**Years made** 2011-
**Engine** V12, 5980cc, twin turbochargers
**Max power** 720bhp @5800rpm
**Torque** 737lb ft @2250-4500rpm
**0-60mph** 3.2sec
**Max speed** 224mph
**Price** c£820,000

**evo** RATING
★★★★★

And the performance is just awe-inspiring. Charging up to 6500rpm in second, your legs go light and your head is pressed hard against the seat. 'Violent' is the best word to sum up a trip from 1500 to 6500rpm in one gear.

The chassis is the perfect ally. Traction is extraordinary and the light, compact drivetrain creates a supreme ability to change direction even when under full attack from the might of the V12.

Seems like Pagani has done it again...

# Panther 6

## QUITE POSSIBLY THE MOST EXTRAORDINARY CAR EVER BUILT, THE SIX-WHEELED PANTHER

Panther never built an ordinary car. From the Jag SS100-aping J72 to the Bugatti Royale-inspired De Ville, the one thing you could always be sure of was that the next Panther would be more outrageous than the last. But nothing could have prepared visitors to the 1977 London Motorfair for the Panther 6. Here was the ultimate supercar as imagined by Panther founder and MD Robert Jankel after seeing the six-wheeled Tyrrell P34 Formula 1 racer at the 1976 British Grand Prix.

Having four front wheels – not to mention being 16 feet long and almost 7 feet wide – assured Panther's wealthiest customers that the 6 would give them all the presence and exclusivity they craved. And the Tyrrell P34's fleeting moment of glory (victory in the 1976 Spanish GP) only served to make the six-wheel concept look like a winner, lending impetus to the notion that this leviathan

SPECIFICATION

**Years made** 1977
**Engine** V8, 8200cc, twin turbochargers
**Max power** 600bhp @5500rpm
**Torque** 600lb ft @2000rpm
**0-60mph** 4.8sec
**Max speed** 200mph
**Price** £39,950 new, c£150,000 today

**evo** RATING
★★★★☆

might indeed be capable of 200mph.

To get the car up to that ambitious 200mph target, Jankel selected the largest engine in production at the time – the 8.2-litre Cadillac Eldorado V8. It was an astute choice. Because the Caddy was front-wheel drive, its engine/gearbox package could be reversed and installed in the back of the Panther 6 for a mid/rear configuration. In truth, the massive powerplant sat slightly behind the axle line, and its high mounting made for a less-than-desirable centre of gravity. In standard form, the huge lump of Detroit iron put out a mere 365bhp, so Jankel got American hot-rod guru Ak Miller to develop a neat-looking twin-turbo arrangement blowing into a single Holley carburettor for a claimed 600bhp.

Unfortunately for Jankel, the dark economic skies of the second energy crisis were looming and, with one production delay after another, the cash finally dried up. Just two Panther 6s are thought to have been built.

Four wheels at the front to do the steering, and an 8.2-litre twin-turbo Caddy V8 in the tail to do the pushing

# Pininfarina Ferrari P4/5

## THE P4/5 IS A ONE-OFF ENZO-BASED SUPERCAR INSPIRED BY CLASSIC 1960s SPORTS RACERS

Ferrari's Enzo is, without doubt, one of the greatest supercars yet seen. Yet for wealthy American collector Jim Glickenhaus it was just the starting point for the car of his dreams. Glickenhaus tracked down the last factory-fresh Enzo on earth and handed it over to Pininfarina with a brief to create a modern evocation of the classic 1960s Ferrari P3/4 sports-racer, an example of which he also owned.

The gorgeous lines of the P4/5 flowed from the pen of Jason Castriota, translated into carbonfibre reality with great attention to the aerodynamics. The finished result was the stunning P4/5, a fully functioning, thoroughly driveable one-off supercar of unique style, and Ferrari itself was so impressed that it gave the project its official approval.

The interior was also radically revamped, the facia incorporating a tablet PC that features not only satnav

### SPECIFICATION

**Years made** 2006
**Engine** V12, 5998cc
**Max power** 660bhp
@ 7800rpm
**Torque** 485lb ft
@ 5500rpm
**0-60mph** 3.0sec
**Max speed** 220mph+
**Price** £4million
(estimated build cost)

### evo RATING
★★★★★

but a 3D model of the car with a parts list and manual to facilitate servicing. Glickenhaus' and his sons' bodies were scanned so that Pininfarina could mould the custom-made seats for their comfort and to provide the optimum view of the road. With 200 new components overall, and all optimised for lightness, the P4/5 managed to shed around 270 kilos from the Enzo's kerb weight.

The mechanical package was left largely untouched, with a marginal increase in power from 650 to 660bhp. Combined with the weight loss, it gave the P4/5 a performance edge over the Enzo, with 0-60 around half a second quicker and a top speed 'in excess of 220mph' where the Enzo topped out at 219mph.

The P4/5 has remained a one-off, though in 2009 Glickenhaus commissioned a race-car from Pininfarina, with similar styling but based on a 430 Scuderia. The P4/5 Competizione finished the 2012 Nürburgring 24-hours a highly creditable 12th overall.

Luca di Montezemolo was so impressed with the P4/5 he gave it Ferrari's official blessing

# Porsche 911 Turbo

## TURBOCHARGING TURNED PORSCHE'S IMMORTAL 911 INTO A BENCHMARK-SETTING SUPERCAR

The 911 Turbo is the car against which the rest of the supercar world calibrates its own ambitions. Back in 1975, when the first 911 Turbo was launched, Porsche purists simply couldn't stand it. They called it fat, lag-prone and a bit flash, choosing to ignore the fact that it was also one of the most devastating supercars of the '70s and, when all said and done, much faster than a 2.7 RS. And destined to get faster.

The 1978 3.3 Turbo was swifter than any of its 911 predecessors and as rapid as anything before the advent of cars like the 959 and Ferrari F40. In its day, the Turbo 3.3 was probably the finest example of precision engineering on four wheels. But the '996' Turbo that arrived at the start of the new millennium was in a different league. By this time – a couple of 911 generations later – the 911 Turbo's power had swollen to 420bhp, which, harnessed to Porsche's terrific

4wd system, delivered 959-challenging acceleration and peerless all-weather point-to-point skills.

And yet, just one decade on (eons in 911 Turbo evolutionary terms) the final iteration of the 997-generation Turbo, the 'S', would blow it into the scenery. With 523bhp and 516lb ft of torque, the Turbo S is as quick to 60mph as a McLaren F1 and only half a nose behind at 100mph. The hugely torquey engine and lightning-fast PDK double-clutch

### SPECIFICATION

**Years made** 1975-
**Engine** Flat-six, 3800cc, twin-turbo (997 Turbo S)
**Max power** 523bhp @ 6250-6750rpm
**Torque** 516lb ft @ 2100-4250rpm
**0-60mph** 3.2sec
**Max speed** 196mph
**Price** £125,865 new, c£80-120,000 used

**evo** RATING
★★★★★

transmission combine to deliver massive, horizon-hauling thrust in return for a modest flexing of your right ankle.

The engine note is more whoosh than wonderful and the whole driving experience lacks the intimate precision, instant agility and bristling tactile and sonic feedback of a GT3's, but there is no denying the Turbo S's blistering pace on any type of road, wet or dry. Or the relatively modest demands on driver talent now needed to achieve it.

By the time the 911 Turbo had reached the 997 generation, the S version was McLaren F1-quick

# Porsche 959

## 911 TAKEN TO THE EXTREME WITH A BARRAGE OF LATE-'80s PERFORMANCE-ENHANCING TECH

**G**ruppe B. That was the name the car that would eventually be known as the 959 wore when it was first presented to the world at the Frankfurt motor show in 1983. A technical tour de force, the car was the brainchild of Porsche's chief engineer, Helmuth Bott, who had proposed a new model for Group B racing. Of course, the fabulous thing about the Group B rules was that they stipulated 200 road-legal examples of a car had to be made for it to be eligible for competition.

And the result was simply the most able supercar of the '80s. It cost as much as a decent house but, for that, you got a car that pulled no punches: it was as good as technology could make it, and that made it a very different proposition to Ferrari's 288 GTO and F40 but, in its own way, just as compelling and exciting.

The size, lightness and engine of the

### SPECIFICATION

**Years made** 1987-1989
**Engine** Flat-six, 2850cc, twin turbochargers
**Max power** 444bhp @6500rpm
**Torque** 369lb ft @5500rpm
**0-60mph** 3.7sec
**Max speed** 197mph
**Price** £150,000 new, £130-£240,000 today

**evo** RATING
★★★★★

911 were important starting points. The compromises inherent in the car's design were exorcised by sheer weight of Porsche engineering, but the compact, quirky cabin, awkward controls and '911-ness' largely remained, as did a flat-six engine installed in what would be most cars' boot.

Computer-controlled four-wheel drive, a six-speed gearbox, a Kevlar and aluminium body, two turbos and 444bhp were what made the 959 such a technical masterpiece. The unrivalled combination of power and traction gave it a 0-60mph time of well under four seconds.

But that was just the party trick. What this Porsche was really good at was distorting conventional frames of reference and notions of what was possible on four wheels. Yes, even now. It actually fulfilled what must have been many a schoolboy's fantasy: to have racing-car performance on regular roads – not just in a straight line, but while cornering and braking, too.

When the twin-turbo, four-wheel-drive 959 appeared in 1987, it made every other supercar look crude and unsophisticated

959 MOT

# Porsche 911 GT1

## WIDER, LONGER, MID-ENGINED, TWIN-TURBO 911 BUILT TO HOMOLOGATE A LE MANS RACER

Porsche and racing: there's a molecular bond. So there was never much doubt that the 911's long and illustrious track career would, at some point, parlay into a pure racing car with number plates to comply with homologation regulations. That car was the 911 GT1 and the year 1996.

Shaken by the success of the McLaren F1 in GT Sportscar racing, not least its overall win at Le Mans, Porsche decided that its response would be a 911-based GT1 car. But turning the 993 GT2 into a Macca slayer wasn't the work of an afternoon. For a start, its engine was in the wrong place. It needed to be in the middle, not at the back, to allow the use of the venturis essential to create sufficient downforce.

Then there was the engine itself: based on the 962 racer's 3.2-litre twin-turbo motor, it developed some 600bhp, comparable to the McLaren's naturally aspirated BMW V12.

Carbonfibre was used for the body – still recognisably 993, albeit longer, lower and festooned with scoops and ducts – and the engineers tried to carry over as much as possible from the regular 911 to reduce costs. Even so, most of the mechanicals had to be created from scratch, including the suspension. But it all worked a treat come the 1996 Le Mans 24hrs, two works cars finishing first and second in class.

In the end, Porsche built 20 GT1s for the road, their engines detuned to 536bhp. The dash was familiar 911 fare, and there was a choice of colours for the leather seats, the exterior paint and even the carpets. Those things apart, though, it was a pure racer: very fast, very loud, very raw and almost impossible to live with - the clutch, for one thing, is so heavy it feels like you're trying to depress the floorpan.

But on the right day, on the right road (or track), it provided a rush like little else.

### SPECIFICATION

**Years made** 1996-98
**Engine** Flat-six, 3163cc, twin turbochargers
**Max power** 536bhp @7000rpm
**Torque** 442lb ft @4250rpm
**0-60mph** 3.6sec
**Max speed** 193mph
**Price** £600,000 new, c£1,000,000 today

**evo RATING**
★★★★☆

Left: now that's what you call a rear wing. GT1 was one of the most extraordinary road-legal vehicles ever produced

# Porsche Carrera GT

## V10-POWERED, CARBON-BODIED AND, WHEN IT ARRIVED IN '04, PORSCHE'S FASTEST SUPERCAR

**S**cintillating as the Carrera GT's performance was (60mph in 3.8sec, 20.4sec for the standing kilometre), it was the race-car purity Porsche was proudest of. In fact, the Carrera GT wasn't a racer lightly modified for the road like the 911 GT1, but a road car derived from racing principles. Which meant it was light as well as powerful. It was also conspicuously low and wide. The deep-slung, mid-mounted engine/transmission kept the centre of gravity within hugging distance of the road. The carbonfibre body that covered it was light and rigid and formed the basis for an innovative safety cage system.

It was the 604bhp, 5.7-litre V10 everyone talked about, though. Its 435lb ft of torque was massive yet the 8200rpm red line extended way into Ferrari Enzo territory. It was all harnessed by a specially developed racing clutch and six-speed transmission. With its

adjustable all-wishbone suspension, forged magnesium wheels and ceramic-composite brakes, it was hard to see anything delivering more potent, hardcore driving thrills.

The Carrera GT was a terrifically engaging car to drive from the moment you depressed the clutch pedal, slotted first and fed in the power. Not that this was a carefree exercise. Coordinating clutch and throttle was a tricky thing to master when pulling away from a standstill. But you immediately sensed the intensity of the Carrera GT's focus. That V10 was an absolute masterpiece, so free-revving and instantaneous, so responsive to the most minute inputs.

It jiggled over bumps and sniffed out cambers, but when you asked everything of the front-end the distractions faded, leaving you with an explicit flow of information. After all, it was a racer at heart, cohesion building in line with your commitment. That's what made it so special, the most special Porsche of all.

Carrera GT was a real drivers' supercar, with on-limit handling that demanded care and commitment. V10 (right) just fab

# Porsche GT2 RS

## A 911 THAT'S QUICKER THAN THE CARRERA GT? THE EXTRAORDINARY GT2 RS IS THAT CAR

The GT2 RS wasn't quicker than a Carrera GT in terms of top speed, of course. That would have been ridiculous. No, flat-out in a straight line it only *matched* Porsche's mid-engined V10 hypercar with an identical 205mph.

Where the RS pulled the Carrera GT's trousers down was where it really mattered – around the Nürburgring, where it was a whole four seconds quicker. Which made it the fastest roadgoing Porsche we'd ever seen.

The 'regular' GT2 was already a turbocharged monster of a 911, but the GT2 RS was something else entirely. Basically it was the chassis of a GT3 RS (the keenest pure driving tool in the Porsche locker) with some modified GT2 aero and a small nuclear device wedge in the orifice between rear axle line and number plate.

So the GT2 RS had a barely conceivable

**SPECIFICATION**

**Years made** 2010-2012
**Engine** Flat-six,
3600cc, twin-turbo
**Max power** 611bhp
@6500rpm
**Torque** 516lb ft
@2250-5500rpm
**0-62mph** 3.5sec
**Max speed** 205mph
**Price** £171,468 new,
c£170,000 used

**evo** RATING
★★★★★

611bhp at its disposal – 88bhp up on the standard GT2 – while the kerbweight had been trimmed by a useful 70kg, giving a power-to-weight ratio of 453bhp per ton. For reference a Ferrari 599 GTO makes 423bhp per ton.

And, of course, the GT2 RS did without the 911 Turbo's four-wheel drive. So how does 611bhp feel when it goes through the rear wheels of a 911? Like a force of nature, as it happens.

In **evo**'s road test, Chris Harris said the only thing he'd driven that was faster from 100-200mph was a Veyron. But he went on to say that the craziest thing about the GT2 RS was that it was so damn useable, a car you could live with every day. 'In short it's a GT3 RS with another 160-odd bhp and a shed-load more torque. It has the steering delicacy, the bump absorption, the ability to communicate, and it just honks between bends like nothing else.'

Limited to just 500 examples, it was no wonder the GT2 RS quickly sold out.

Above: under all the carbon intake ducting was the most powerful Porsche road car engine yet

# Porsche 918 Spyder

## THE HYBRID-POWERED SUCCESSOR TO THE CARRERA GT IS CAPABLE OF 202MPH OR 94MPG

In November 2013, supercar reality (as opposed to conceptual fantasising) undergoes a step-change that will have anti-car lobbyists spluttering into their breakfasts. Because that's when Porsche's 918 Spyder – the stunning hybrid supercar that dropped jaws at the 2010 Geneva motor show – goes on sale and the notion that supercars are unsupportable on the grounds of their inherent profligacy is shattered.

Working together, the 918's V8 petrol engine and brace of electric motors will deliver 795bhp. Nothing too unusual there for a car designed to fill the role vacated by the Carrera GT in Porsche's model range. No, the killer stats are these: an official economy figure of 94mpg (more than any current UK production car, Prius included) and $CO_2$ emissions of 70g/km, which under current regs equates to free UK road tax.

**SPECIFICATION**

**Years made** 2013-
**Engine** V8, 4600cc, plus
two electric motors
**Max power** 795bhp
combined
**Torque** 575lb ft
@1000-4000rpm
**0-60mph** 3.0sec
**Max speed** 202mph
**Price** £672,000

**evo** RATING
★★★★½

It will come as no comfort to the eco police that this paragon of parsimony will rocket to 60mph in 3.0sec and reach 202mph, or that it recently completed a lap of the Nordschleife in 7min 14sec, even if they knew what the Nordschleife was. (That time beat the GT2 RS, hitherto the fastest Porsche, by a full 4sec, the Carrera GT by a massive 17sec.)

The 918's mid-mounted, high-revving V8 is based on the RS Spyder racing car's engine and will put out around 580bhp. It drives the rear wheels through a seven-speed PDK twin-clutch gearbox, while the electric motors – one each on the front and rear axles – contribute around 150bhp each to the total. This effectively makes the 918 Spyder all-wheel drive.

The Spyder can even be driven around 20 miles on electric power alone and its lithium-ion battery can be charged from domestic power sockets. All that tech adds up to a 1700kg kerbweight, and doesn't come cheap. But then game-changing technology seldom is.

Martini livery on this final prototype is a nod to classic Porsches, but the 918 is a pure road car and a taste of the future

# Ruf CTR 'Yellow Bird'

## TO THOSE IN THE KNOW IN THE LATE 1980s, THIS 911-BASED ROAD-ROCKET WAS A LEGEND

**B**efore the Bugatti Veyron, before the McLaren F1, the Ruf CTR was probably the most famous fast car in the world. Not famous in the sense that it was a household name ('A Ruf Porsche? What's the matter with it?') but celebrated, almost beatified, by a small band of enthusiasts who knew how extraordinary it was.

They christened it 'Yellow Bird' – mostly, one assumes, because the first one made was yellow and because Yellow Bird sounded vaguely mythic, anyway. And justly so because the Ruf – essentially a heavily re-engineered 911 with twin turbos and the best part of 500bhp – soon took its first step to becoming a legend in the hands of an American magazine at Ehra Lessien, VW's superfast test track near the east German border. The event was a no-bullshit face-off between a dozen of the world's fastest cars. The CTR blew

### SPECIFICATION

**Years made** 1987-1991
**Engine** Flat-6, 3600cc, twin turbochargers
**Max power** 469bhp @ 5950rpm
**Torque** 408lb ft @ 5100rpm
**0-60mph** 4.1sec
**Max speed** 211mph
**Price** c£185,000 new, £150-200,000 today

### evo RATING
★★★★★

them all away – Porsche's 959 included – with a top speed of 211.5mph. The CTR, you see, wasn't just a 911 Turbo with topped-up testosterone. It was a 911 Turbo with expletives included.

The point was rammed home by Ruf's subsequent promo video, shot mostly from a helicopter, in which Yellow Bird and *Auto Motor und Sport* tester (then Ruf employee) Stefan Roser lapped the Nürburgring in a continuous, jaw-dropping, tyre-melting power slide.

Yellow Bird was a purification of Porsche-ness, a concentration of the things that define a 911. That amazing size-to-speed ratio, the intensity and resolution of tactile and aural feedback (helm, suspension, engine sound), the oversteer...

Ruf's philosophy was to pare and harden until all the frills and peripheral distractions had been excised. Honesty: rear-wheel drive, 500 horses, steering wheel, throttle, brake pedal. Either you could hack the CTR or you couldn't.

Alois Ruf's company comprehensively re-engineered the 911 and added twin turbos to create the Yellow Bird legend

# **Ruf** R Turbo

## *BRIEFLY THE WORLD'S FASTEST CAR – BUT THERE WAS SO MUCH MORE TO THE R TURBO*

**B**ack in 2001, the Ruf R Turbo had the highest independently verified top speed of any new car in the world, at 213mph. A few years later, Bugatti launched a car that would go 50mph faster.

In fact the arrival of the Veyron did Ruf a huge favour, shifting the faintly ludicrous obsession with top speed onto another level and allowing Ruf to be appreciated for the full extent of its products' talents rather than an eye-catching headline.

A little history. The first Ruf-enhanced Porsche appeared in 1975, and the company's first complete model arrived in 1977, a tuned 930-generation 911 with its flat-six stroked to 3.3 litres. Over the years the company has built many widely celebrated supercars, and these days Ruf Automobile GmbH, still run by Alois Ruf jnr, is classed as a manufacturer in its own right.

The joy of the early Rufs was their understatement; only the aficionado would know that they were looking at one of the world's fastest and greatest supercars. And the 996-based R Turbo, like the CTR models before it, was so much more than a pumped-up 911.

As was Ruf's wont, it deliberately looked somewhat dressed down – especially in Alois Ruf's favoured, performance-massaging, narrow-bodied guise. Certainly, there was nothing on the outside to broadcast 0-60mph in 3.7sec or 0-100mph in 7.9sec – and that in basic 520bhp tune (it was also offered with 550 and 590bhp). The Ruf was far stealthier than any GT3 or GT2.

The R Turbo represented a greater concentration of repacked Porsche-ness than anything Ruf had done to date. It was also faster and more rewarding than Porsche's own GT2 of the day. Ruf's policy was to distill all the core 911 virtues so that all that was left was the driving. The R Turbo illustrated it perfectly.

At a time when factory 911s were losing a little of their raw appeal, Ruf was building undiluted driving machines

# Ruf Rt 12

*ANOTHER GENERATION OF 911 SAW THE ARRIVAL OF ANOTHER SCINTILLATING RUF...*

**R**uf's take on the 997-generation 911 was the Rt 12. Unsurprisingly it was the fastest Ruf yet, and as with the previous Turbo R (996) and CTR-2 (993), the formula for lifting its performance from stock Porsche to the top tier of the world's fastest cars was much the same.

Despite the new 997 platform, Ruf stuck with a twin-turbocharged 3.6 based on the previous 996-series Turbo engine. Customers could choose how much power they required to scare themselves silly (530 or 560bhp usually did the job) and whether to stick with Porsche's all-wheel drive or have all the power directed to the rear wheels, which, incidentally, turned out to be by far the more popular option.

For the truly dedicated, Ruf also offered a 3.8-litre S version with 685bhp. No doubt spurred on by the exploits of former employee Jan Fatthauer over at 9ff (see p218), the Rt 12 with optional 'long' gearing had a claimed top speed of 227mph and a 9.7sec 0-200kph (124mph) time.

On the move, the Rt 12 feels deeply impressive, the structure reinforced with a neatly integrated roll-cage, the ride supple, huge wheels and tyres tightly controlled by bespoke Bilstein dampers and Eibach springs.

As with all Rufs, the engine is wonderfully tractable, but when you squeeze the throttle harder the power

## SPECIFICATION

**Years made** 2004-
**Engine** Flat-six, 3746cc, twin-turbo (Rt 12 S)
**Max power** 685bhp @7000rpm
**Torque** 649lb ft @4000rpm
**0-60mph** 3.4sec
**Max speed** 227mph
**Price** c£155,000 new, c£100-£150,000 today

**evo** RATING
★★★★★

swells inexorably, acceleration coming in a torrent. At full thrust, the occupants feel like astronauts at lift-off.

Of course you have to treat it with huge respect, especially if you're driving the rear-wheel drive version, and particularly if you're brave enough to switch out the PSM. This is not a car to power-slide for fun. It's not often the road testers at **evo** say this, but in the case of the Ruf Rt 12, for once we'd be tempted to take the four-wheel-drive version...

Rt 12's rear wings were wider than a Porsche Turbo's; door mirrors were smaller to cut drag

# Ruf CTR3

## THE ULTIMATE RUF IS A 740BHP MID-ENGINED RIVAL TO THE LIKES OF THE ENZO AND ZONDA

**R**he Ruf CTR3 is the car that Alois Ruf has wanted to make ever since taking the reins of the Pfaffenhausen-based company in 1974: a no-compromise, premier-league supercar designed from the ground up. Not one saddled with the rear-slung engine of the 911, nor a modified edition of the mid-engined Cayman with a ridiculous amount of power. No, a true Enzo-class mid-engined

exotic that, apart from anything else, would fill the void left by Porsche's own 'best game' but defunct contender, the Carrera GT. In fact, as well as exceeding the ambition of the original 469bhp CTR 'Yellow Bird' and the 520bhp CTR2 that followed a decade later, the CTR3 reached beyond even that of the CGT.

The Ruf CTR3 has 740bhp and a claimed top speed of 236mph, a breezy 16mph clear of a Ferrari Enzo's. Only a tiny group of production supercars

## SPECIFICATION

**Years made** 2009-
**Engine** Flat-six, 3746cc, twin turbochargers
**Max power** 740bhp @ 7600rpm
**Torque** 705lb ft @ 4000rpm
**0-60mph** 3.2sec
**Max speed** 236mph
**Price** £357,000 new, c£300,000 used

**evo** RATING
★★★★★

are faster, and then not by much. But that didn't concern Alois Ruf. Chasing the biggest figures has never been an obsession for him. Like Gordon Murray said of the McLaren F1, the astonishing performance was a consequence of the car's design and engineering, not its aim.

The twin-turbo flat-six engine was essentially the same motor as in the Rt 12 but producing 740bhp at 7600rpm and 705lb ft of torque at 4000rpm, all directed to the rear wheels via a six-speed sequential transmission built by Hor.

There's no haymaker to the kidneys. Just a push that builds with the relentless intensity of an avalanche. The interesting stuff happens between 100 and 200mph, the zone that separates the true hardware from chip-tweaked pretension, the zone where the Ruf hits its natural stride. The sustained, broadband ferocity of the acceleration is something you'd need to spend many hours, days, getting used to. It's a thoroughly convincing supercar, the best car Porsche never made.

Left: CTR3's mid-engined layout is obvious from the rear. Quality of materials is first-rate

# Saleen S7

There's something of a tradition in the US for successful tuners – having tuned the hell out of any number of muscle-cars – to grab a clean sheet of paper and craft a machine to fully exploit their go-faster talents. Back at the start of the new millennium, Michigan-based Steve Saleen (specialist subject: turning Mustangs into racers) was such a man and the Saleen (Jim Carey's wheels of choice when he became God in the movie Bruce Almighty) was such a car.

Five years later, the Saleen had become the most successful road-going supercar-based racer ever. (Naturally, given his background, Mr S offered racing versions from the start.) All right, it was a comparatively low-tech affair with a rather extravagant and over-styled glassfibre and carbon body over a steel tube chassis and a huge 7.0-litre Ford pushrod V8 sitting just in front of the

### SPECIFICATION

**Years made** 2005-2009
**Engine** V8, 6998cc, twin turbochargers (S7)
**Max power** 750bhp @6300rpm
**Torque** 700lb ft @4800rpm
**0-60mph** 2.8sec
**Max speed** 248mph
**Price** c£350,000 new, c£200-£250,000 used

**evo RATING**
★★★★☆

rear axle. But then that was the good ol' mend-it-with-a-hammer American Way.

As the S7 version, with a brace of turbos bolted on, the Saleen cranked out 750bhp – enough, it was claimed, to go sub 3sec to 60mph and get within sneezing distance of 250mph. There was even talk of a 1000bhp version. Sadly, Saleen ceased trading in 2009, but it had been quite a ride.

To drive, the S7 was as raw and challenging as you'd imagine. The racing clutch was tricky to get off the line smoothly, the huge body made it tricky to place, the suspension transmitted every jolt. But given some space and a decent surface it was easy to make absurdly fast progress. With 448bhp per ton, it just exploded forward at almost any speed and any revs, while the steering was so instantly responsive it took a while to become accustomed to it. At high speed you could feel the aerodynamic downforce pressing the S7 against the tarmac. A racing car for the road? You bet.

Huge Ford pushrod V8 (right) with twin turbos, and an outsize carbon- and glassfibre body: a supercar US-style

# SSC Ultimate Aero

## THE CAR THAT OUT-RAN THE VEYRON AND FORCED BUGATTI TO BUILD THE SUPER SPORT

**C**ar guys in high places are a competitive bunch. When VW Group boss Ferdinand Piëch gave the green light to the Bugatti Veyron, he could have been forgiven for thinking 'well, that's that then'. But, phenomenal as the Veyron's performance was, that, most definitely, was not that.

The Veyron may well have been one supercar to rule them all, but its performance stats were there to be shot down. First to make no bones about its intention to do just that was Jerod Shelby (no relation to Carroll) with a product that might have been mistaken for an overrated chocolate bar but which, on September 13, 2007, stuck it to the Bug by recording a top speed of 256.19mph, a feat later recognised by Guinness as a new fastest production car world record.

Despite looking like the sort of generic, non-specific supercar an advertising agency might have knocked up in an afternoon to sell car polish, the Aero, as its name suggests, was a slippery thing. If you can see hints of Diablo, that's no coincidence. Shelby SuperCars started out building Lambo replicas, and the spaceframe formed the basis for the Ultimate Aero prototype.

Power came from what has become GM's gift to America's bash-the-Bug club: a Corvette V8, with two XXL turbos. Low-tech it may be, but the seemingly indestructible pushrod motor can be persuaded to give up quite ridiculous amounts of power and torque without infringing emissions regs and is undoubtedly the most prolific and cost-effective 1000bhp+ engine on the planet. Consider that it took the £2m Veyron Super Sport to wrest the 'world's fastest' title back from the Ultimate Aero with a top speed of 267.86mph.

It isn't over, of course. The next SSC, the Tuatara, is said to have 1350bhp, with a projected top speed of 276mph. It's a silly game, but we like it.

**SPECIFICATION**

**Years made** 2006-
**Engine** V8, 6342cc, twin turbochargers
**Max power** 1183bhp @6950rpm
**Torque** 1094lb ft @6150rpm
**0-60mph** 2.8sec
**Max speed** 256mph
**Price** c£417,000 new, c£300,000 used

**evo** RATING
★★★★☆

Many supercars claim outrageous top speeds, but few have them confirmed by Guinness. This is the actual 256mph SSC

# Sportec SPR1 M

## THERE ARE TUNED 911 TURBOS, AND THEN THERE'S THE STUPENDOUS SPORTEC SPR1 M

I t's a 911. But not as we know it. Standard 911 Turbos don't come out of the factory with carbon-Kevlar bodywork. They aren't born with a secondary safety cage, two injectors per cylinder and titanium conrods either. Above all, Weissach doesn't equip them with the firepower to see off a Veyron.

Enter the Swiss-made Sportec SPR1 M with 846bhp and a claimed 240mph+ top speed. The pursuit of speed and speed alone is not the Sportec's sole aim, though. Instead think of it as the ultimate 911 Turbo, the sort of bespoke creation that former Porsche CEO Wendelin Wiedeking might have hoped to receive as a leaving gift when he retired – but probably didn't.

A quick prod of the calculator reveals the Sportec almost doubles the standard Turbo's power-to-weight. At 593bhp per ton it's also 72bhp per ton up on the Veyron. It feels like a Turbo that's

Top: no outlandish bodywork, just a subtly pumped-up stance that hints at the massive power contained within

### SPECIFICATION

**Years made** 2009-
**Engine** Flat-six, 3600cc, twin-turbo
**Max power** 846bhp @8200rpm
**Torque** 642lb ft @4800rpm
**0-60mph** 3.0sec
**Max speed** 240mph+
**Price** £500,000 (plus donor car!)

**evo** RATING
★★★★☆

been condensed, distilled, and had all its impurities removed. Fact is, no Turbo has ever had a more talkative, precise front end, nor delivered such steering clarity, nor built so much ride tolerance into so little travel. And perhaps the best thing of all is that it's really quite subtle.

It's a gorgeous thing, the Sportec – a hypercar you can work with, a Veyron without the baggage and numbness, a vice-free any-occasion rocketship with a low radar reflection.

# Spyker C8 Aileron

## AN INTRIGUING MIX OF FANTASY AND HARDCORE, THE C8 AILERON IS SERIOUSLY GOOD

The Spyker name was resurrected in 2000 – 102 years after it had first been associated with a motor car – by Dutch tycoon Victor Muller, who established the new Spyker company in Zeewolde, Holland. Described by some as a Dutch pocket-sized Zonda, the first new-era Spyker – the mid-engined C8 Laviolette of 2001 – evolved into the longer, prettier and (with the help of Lotus) more dynamically sussed Aileron. It still looked like a renegade concept exhibit, mind.

For such a comparatively compact car, the Aileron's presence is colossal, a hyperactive mélange of scoops, vents, 'aeroblade' wheels, upswinging doors and conspicuously crafted body jewellery. Inside, the aesthetic onslaught is even more intense, spearheaded, without a doubt, by the naked and gleaming gear-linkage that runs almost the entire length of the cabin, though the equally exposed

**SPECIFICATION**

**Years made** 2009-
**Engine** V8, 4163cc
**Max power** 400bhp
@ 6800rpm
**Torque** 354lb ft
@ 3500rpm
**0-60mph** 4.4sec
**Max speed** 187mph
**Price** c£191,000 new,
c£90-£150,000 used

**evo** RATING
★★★★☆

pedal assembly, seemingly hewn from solid aluminium, comes a close second.

Powered by a tuned Audi 4.2-litre V8 developing 400bhp, mated to a ZF six-speed automatic, the drivetrain, in contrast, is rather run-of-the-mill but ideal for the job: compact, light and muscular. Besides, there's nothing wrong with having an Audi engine. So does the Lamborghini Gallardo and Bugatti Veyron.

As with the C8 Laviolette, the Aileron is an odd but curiously intoxicating mixture of fantasy and hardcore that goes like stink, handles with track-car-aping acuity and presses all the right supercar buttons, plus a few more.

In 2010, production moved to the UK, with Coventry-based company CPP engaged to construct the Aileron. Unfortunately the future of Spyker Cars looks far from certain. Its history has been a rollercoaster – at one point it owned an F1 team – and there have been a number of attempts to sell the marque, but the most recent deal fell through.

Left: like a Dutch pocket Zonda. Above: even Zondas can't out-dazzle the Spyker's interior

# Tramontana R Edition

## SPANISH-MADE, MERCEDES V12-POWERED AND UTTERLY BONKERS, THAT'S THE TRAMONTANA

Josep Rubau never wanted to build just another generic supercar with a smattering of Ferrari at the front and Lamborghini at the rear. The Royal College of Art graduate set out to make a statement, to build a car that would sell to just a few people a year. With the Tramontana R, you'd probably say it's mission accomplished.

The bizarre, Spanish-built Tramontana is part supercar, part F1, and part jet-fighter with its wrap-around canopy. It's powered by a twin-turbo 5.5-litre Mercedes V12 and takes just 10.1sec to hit 125mph from rest. It is also said to be capable of more than 1.22g through corners. Get past the oddball looks, and it calls to mind another small-volume hypercar, the Pagani Zonda.

Given its head, the R is truly ferocious. Its unique layout only adds to the sensation of speed: sitting high over the

nose, it feels like a 200mph, warm, dry motorcycle ride. Add the intoxicating note of the engine, steering so direct it feels almost like an extension of your arms, and every piece of racing tech that could possibly cross over, and you have a recipe for something quite extraordinary.

Underneath the challenging exterior is a wealth of engineering depth, from the carbonfibre chassis to the fully adjustable Ohlins horizontal dampers with their external reservoirs. A sequential gearshift operates a six-speed Cima 'box. In-line seats keep the weight over the centre-line, though if you take a passenger they had better be a close friend, because rubbing legs is a standard part of the Tramontana experience.

It's an automotive oddball all right, and with prices from around half a million euros, it'll always be one of the rarest of all supercars – Rubau says he will never build more than a dozen examples a year. But if supercars are all about creating shockwaves, few do it better.

Tramontana started life as an open-topped supercar, then gained the forward-hinging canopy (left) for the R Edition

S 7·339 BBR

# TVR Speed 12

## THE CAR THAT, LEGEND HAS IT, BROKE THE ENGINE DYNO: THE MONSTER 7.7-LITRE SPEED 12

The uber-TVR first saw light of day as Project 7/12, which debuted at the 1996 Birmingham motor show and caused a sensation. Its monster engine was essentially two Cerbera straight-sixes spliced together to make a 7.7-litre V12 developing... well, that's always been the matter of some conjecture. The story goes that it snapped the input shaft of TVR's 1000bhp-rated dyno. When the engineers then measured each bank of cylinders separately at 480bhp, a rough estimate of 960bhp was suggested, though the figure eventually quoted 'officially' by TVR was 800bhp.

The finished design was ready in 2000, along with a racing version for the GT2 class. The racer would go on to win several rounds in British GTs, though it was dogged with reliability problems. Its reputation as a dyno-killer can't have done it any harm, though, and despite a

**SPECIFICATION**

**Years made** 2000
**Engine** V12, 7730cc
**Max power** 800bhp
@ 8250rpm
**Torque** 650lb ft
@ 5750rpm
**0-60mph** 3.0sec
**Max speed** 200mph+
**Price** £188,000
(list price in 2000)

**evo** RATING
★★★★½

list price of £188,000 the deposits for the road car began to pile up.

But then TVR boss Peter Wheeler took one of the finished prototypes home for the night and, on his return, declared it too powerful and wild for the road. And so production plans for a TVR that could take down a McLaren F1 were canned, deposits returned and the remaining prototypes broken up for spares to service the remaining race cars.

Except for one. In August 2003, TVR placed an ad for a Speed 12 with the registration W112 BHG, to be sold to an enthusiast personally vetted by Wheeler. It would combine the one remaining road car prototype with the bodyshell from one of the GT racers. One obvious bonus was that it would have downforce aero. Another was that its new owner was happy for evo's John Barker to drive it. Supercar 'hands' don't come much more seasoned than JB and he memorably summed-up the Speed 12's acceleration in one word: terrifying.

Left: TVR DNA just about visible under the aero of the race-car bodyshell. Right: now that's what you call road presence

# TVR Typhon

## EXOTIC CONSTRUCTION AND ULTRA RARITY MAKE THE TYPHON ONE VERY SPECIAL TVR

The need for speed was never far from TVR boss Peter Wheeler's thoughts. So even though the dyno-snapping Speed 12 gave him a temporary reality check, it wasn't long after its demise that the old itch kicked in again. The result was a sort of pumped-up Tuscan, initially known as the Tuscan R (or T440R) before the name Typhon was settled upon.

Prototypes used the 400bhp naturally-aspirated Speed Six engine from the Tuscan S, but the idea was to supercharge it for a target output of 580bhp, giving the Typhon a better power-to-weight ratio than a Ferrari Enzo, a claim supported by the step-change in construction the Typhon represented. Designed from the ground up using CAD (a first for TVR), it would have a steel spaceframe with full roll-cage, incorporating aluminium honeycomb sections and a carbonfibre floor.

**SPECIFICATION**

**Years made** 2006
**Engine** In-line 6-cyl, 3996cc
**Max power** 400bhp @ 7000rpm
**Torque** 330lb ft @ 5250rpm
**0-60mph** 3.9sec
**Max speed** 190mph+
**Price** £84,995 new, c£100,000 today

**evo RATING**
★★★★☆

Wheeler even suggested that the differential and driveshafts that had been developed for the Speed 12 could have a home in the Typhon. But they would have been rather wasted on the standard T400-spec engines that ended up in the two Typhons that were eventually built after Wheeler had sold up to the young Russian tycoon Nikolai Smolenski.

*evo* drove one of these Typhons in 2007, shortly after Smolenski had ominously halted production at the factory. We found it light, stiff, quick, challenging and hugely exciting. 'There are moments when no other car could match the involvement and sheer excitement it serves up,' we said. 'If the TVR story ends here, the Typhon will serve as a reminder that its demise was never about a lack of talent or skill in Blackpool.'

The supercharged engine and planned hydraulically actuated sequential gearbox were never finished. Soon after, however, TVR was. Sad to say, we'll probably never see the Typhon's like again.

Left and opposite: though clearly related to the Tuscan, the lighter, faster Typhon was a very different sort of animal

# Ultima GTR640/720

**A**rguably the most underrated car on the planet, the Ultima GTR has a bang-for-buck quotient most supercar makers wouldn't think possible or, indeed, desirable. Thing is, Ted Marlow, boss of Leicestershire-based Ultima, has never been interested in exotic styling, fancy interiors or seeing how much he could charge for a car that does 230mph. He's just interested in making the quickest and most capable road-cum-trackday car in the world and selling it for a realistic price – or in kit form for even less.

Evolved out of an original Lee Noble (clearly Group C racer-inspired) design in 1983, today's Ultima GTR doesn't look a whole lot different. The body hangs on a tubular spaceframe and suspension is by double wishbones front and rear.

What's changed most over the years has been the power. It's hard to believe the first Ultimas were propelled by a Ford Capri-issue 'Essex' V6. In its most potent form, the GTR comes with a 6.2-litre Chevy V8 developing either 641 or 720bhp (or, if you really insist, even more). In a car that weighs just 980 kilos, well, the Ultima's potential for reddening the faces of Ferrari, Porsche and even Veyron drivers is obvious: 0-60mph in 2.6sec, 0-100mph 5.3sec, and 0-100-0mph 9.4sec. Which happened to be a world record.

It's not just about the performance though. On a challenging road you can feel the chassis working beneath you, gauge the level of grip through the rim of the wheel and the seat of your pants, and exploit that grip to whatever extent you're comfortable with.

There's no electronic traction control, no anti-lock, now power steering – and you know what? You don't miss them. The GTR is every bit as rewarding – and certainly every bit as quick – as its Group C styling suggests. As the Americans would say, it walks the talk.

## SPECIFICATION

**Years made** 1999-
**Engine** V8, 7011cc
**Max power** 720bhp @6500rpm
**Torque** 560lb ft @4800rpm
**0-60mph** 2.6sec
**Max speed** 231mph
**Price** c£68,000 new, £40-60,000 used

### evo RATING
★★★★½

Left: nothing fancy about the Ultima, just well-proven components that add up to one of the world's fastest cars

# Vector W8

THE TWIN-TURBO VECTOR W8 WAS CONCEIVED TO BE AMERICA'S ANSWER TO LAMBORGHINI

Of all the supercars given to a bit of aerospace posturing – the Bristol Fighter and Lambo Reventón are recent examples that spring to mind – the Vector W8 arguably took the biscuit. The brainchild of Gerry Wiegert, who founded his Vector Aeromotive company in 1971, the W8 was an awful long time in the making, evolving out of the engine-less Vector show car and prototype W2

and eventually breaking cover in 1989 before breaking down, in one widely reported incident, with its new owner, tennis star Andre Agassi, at the wheel. Aside from its sensational appearance – which would comfortably out-wow most current Lamborghinis and Ferraris – the Vector's USP was its aircraft-grade materials and construction which, in no small part, contributed to its outrageous $455,000 price tag.

Still, the 17 people who wrote the

SPECIFICATION

Years made 1989-1993
Engine V8, 5973cc,
twin turbochargers
Max power 625bhp
@ 5700rpm
Torque 630lb ft
@ 4900rpm
0-60mph 4.2sec
Max speed 220mph
Price c£275,000
($455,000) new,
c£150-200,000 today

evo RATING
★★★☆☆

cheque wouldn't have been disappointed with the performance. The W8's 6-litre V8 had forged aluminium pistons, a forged crankshaft, twin turbochargers, electronic direct port fuel injection, 625bhp and 630lb ft of torque. The claimed top speed was 220mph, with 0-60mph in 4.2sec despite the W8 having a three-speed auto gearbox.

Next up was the 1993 WX-3, which was to have 1200bhp. But before anything could come of it, Indonesian company Mega Tech, which owned Lamborghini at the time, acquired a controlling interest in Vector, fired Wiegert and went on to produce the Lambo V12-engined M12 instead. Which no one bought.

After a court battle, Wiegert won back the rights to Vector in 2008 and revealed that he was developing a new supercar called the WX-8. With a 10-litre turbocharged V8, it would have 1800bhp, giving a projected top speed of 300mph. Little has been seen or heard of it since, but it's early days...

Above: Vector's USP was aircraft-grade materials and construction, while a twin-turbo V8 gave a claimed 220mph

# Yamaha OX99-11

The closest you will get to driving a Formula 1 car on the road. That was the unique proposition of the Yamaha OX99-11. Though the rival McLaren had the 'F1' name, there was no question which of the two was more closely related to real Grand Prix machinery. In fact, if you imagined the major components of an F1 car with an aluminium skin wrapped round them, you were pretty close to the OX99-11.

Yamaha was an established F1 engine builder in the late 1980s and early '90s, but for its road car project it formed a technical alliance with British design and development company IAD. The resulting vehicle was unlike anything before or since. Like the McLaren F1, it sat the driver plumb in the centre. And thanks to the jet fighter-style bubble canopy, forward visibility was absolutely brilliant. Rearwards? Didn't really matter. Within inches of the backrest was a detuned

version of the 3.5-litre Yamaha V12 fitted to the Brabhams and Jordans of the early 1990s, developing 420bhp at an eye-watering 10,000rpm. Like the driver, it sat in a carbonfibre monocoque chassis.

The bodyshell that clothed it was lean, compact and functional with some very serious-looking aero. It was fashioned from hand-beaten alloy, ostensibly to add the right degree of bespoke exclusivity, though the carbon moulding techniques of the day weren't really up to coping with the complex curves of the design. The OX99-11 had a projected top speed of 200mph with 0-60 in 3.7sec. The price was a cool $1million, or around £600,000 at the exchange rates of the day.

It just didn't add up. The looks divided opinion; in testing the car was found to be heavily compromised for road use – heavy steering, twitchy handling, raucous engine – the price was putting off potential buyers, and with development costs spiralling the project was canned with just three prototypes completed.

## SPECIFICATION

**Years made** 1992 (prototypes only)
**Engine** V12, 3498cc
**Max power** 420bhp @ 10,000rpm
**Torque** n/a
**0-60mph** 3.7sec
**Max speed** 200mph
**Price** c£600,000 new

### evo RATING
★★★★☆

One of the most intriguing of all supercar projects, the F1-based Yamaha sadly never made it into production

# Zenvo ST1

## *A DANISH SUPERCAR TO RIVAL THE GREATS? THE ZENVO SHAPES UP SURPRISINGLY WELL*

**D**anish company Zenvo Automotive was founded in 2004 with the express intent of creating a world-class supercar, and in 2009 it revealed the result: the extremely striking and stupendously powerful ST1, boasting a Bugatti-bothering 1104bhp.

That astonishing power figure is produced by a 16-valve, 7-litre V8, based on the architecture of a GM unit but recreated in alloy with dry-sump lubrication and bespoke crank, rods and forged pistons, and both supercharged and turbocharged. It drives the rear wheels via a conventional six-speed manual gearbox (a seven-speed paddleshift box is an option), with a limited-slip diff and traction control to prevent all that bhp vapourising the massive 335/30 x 20in rear Michelin Pilot Sports. Suspension is double wishbones all round, with adjustable Ohlins dampers. That's classic race-car practice, as are the

| SPECIFICATION | |
|---|---|
| Years made | 2010- |
| Engine | V8, 7000cc, s/charger & turbo |
| Max power | 1104bhp @6900rpm |
| Torque | 1053lb ft @4500rpm |
| 0-60mph | 3.0sec |
| Max speed | 233mph |
| Price | c800,000 euros new |

**evo** RATING
★★★★½

steel spaceframe and carbonfibre panels. But then the ST1 also has speed-sensitive power steering and anti-lock brakes.

Zenvo's aim was to build a car that combined extraordinary performance with genuine useability and cutting-edge design, and early drives of the final prototypes suggested it had succeeded, with a surprising degree of tractability and civility. The cockpit is lavishly equipped, and options include a fitted luggage set as well as a roll-cage and four-point harnesses. Then you open the taps and other-worldly acceleration comes in a torrent, accompanied by a bellowing, unashamedly macho soundtrack.

Always intended as a showcase for its talents and as a strictly limited edition, Zenvo says a maximum of 15 ST1s will be built. Doesn't sound like many, but as plenty of others have discovered, it's one thing to create a supercar, quite another to find buyers and turn it into a successful business. From what we've seen, Zenvo stands a better chance than many.

Above and right: ST1 styling is both cohesive and distinctive. Left: detailing is neat, the cabin well-finished

# 9ff GT9R

## THE MID-ENGINED PORSCHE-BASED GT9R IS ONE OF THE FASTEST CARS WE'VE EVER DRIVEN

**I**t's don't be afraid, be very afraid time. Anyone who has followed the career of Dortmund-based Jan Fatthauer will know why. The estimable Herr Fatthauer once worked for Ruf. This undoubtedly gave him a taste of how Porsches, especially 911s, could be reworked into faster and more formidable versions of their former selves. But not fast or formidable enough, apparently. In 2001 he left to form his own Porsche reimagining outfit, 9ff, in order to push the envelope a little further. Or quite a lot further as it turned out. 911s with eye-popping outputs and top speeds ensued.

Then, as they say, he went for it. The Veyron has got a lot to answer for. The GT9R is the 'hot' version of a car – to be brutally honest, an elongated, uglified 911 with its engine repositioned in the middle called the GT9 – that already had 987bhp, a claimed top speed of 254mph and 100mph-plus roll-on acceleration to

overhaul the celebrated million-quid Bug. The 'R' just kind of rubbed it in for 20 lucky people with a mind to do so. And with 1120bhp and a claimed 260mph maximum in their goodie bag, there isn't much holding them back. Let's hope they pack some of those famous 'brave pills'.

When **evo**'s Roger Green drove the GT9 at Bruntingthorpe in 2008, he hit 221.9mph – at the time the fastest speed recorded by a road car in the UK – before running out of space. And that was just

the basic car. The R version above is just plain bonkers: above 100mph it eats Veyrons for breakfast, accelerating from 100 to 200mph a full 2.5 seconds quicker than the Bug.

Perhaps equally remarkably, the GT9R is disarmingly easy to drive slowly – certainly no more demanding than a 911 GT3 – with a progressive, medium-weight clutch, easy gearchange and well-weighted, communicative steering. The calm before the storm...

**SPECIFICATION**

**Years made** 2008-
**Engine** Flat-6-cyl, 4000cc, twin turbochargers
**Max power** 1120bhp @7850rpm
**Torque** 774lb ft @5970rpm
**0-60mph** 2.9sec
**Max speed** 250mph+
**Price** c£450,000 new

**evo** RATING
★★★★½